Quick scan of post 9/11 national counter-terrorism policymaking and implementation in selected European countries

Research project for the Netherlands Ministry of Justice

MR - 1590
May 2002

Erik van de Linde, Kevin O'Brien, Gustav Lindstrom,
Stephan de Spiegeleire, Mikko Vayrynen and Han de Vries

RAND *Europe*

The research described in this report was prepared for the Netherlands Ministry of Justice.

ISBN: 0-8330-3265-8

Published 2002 by RAND
1700 Main Street, P.O. Box 2138, Santa Monica, CA 90407-2138
1200 South Hayes Street, Arlington, VA 22202-5050
201 North Craig Street, Suite 202, Pittsburgh, PA 15213-1516
RAND URL: http://www.rand.org/
To order RAND documents or to obtain additional information, contact Distribution Services: Telephone: (310) 451-7002; Fax: (310) 451-6915; Email: order@rand.org

Acknowledgements

We would like to thank the Dutch Ministry of Justice for the opportunity to perform this quick scan. Also, we would like to thank government officials in The Netherlands, Belgium, Finland, France, Germany, Spain and the United Kingdom for taking the time to talk to us and to provide us with documentation where appropriate.

We also thank Ian Lesser and David Gompert of RAND and RAND Europe for the valuable advise they gave us concerning the methodology and the content of the quick scan.

Finally, Michael Wermuth of RAND is acknowledged for his quality assessment of the report.

Further information about this project can be obtained from the authors.

RAND Europe
Phone +31 71 5245151
Fax +31 71 5245199
e-mail reinfo@rand.org

Leiden, May 2002

Preface

A comparative analysis of The Netherlands, Belgium, Finland, France, Germany, Spain and the United Kingdom was performed with respect to their counter-terrorism policymaking and implementation following the 11 September 2001 terrorist attacks on the New York World Trade Centre and the Pentagon and the crash of the hijacked airplane in Pennsylvania.

The goal of the comparative analysis was to make a contribution to improving coordination of counter-terrorism among European Union Member States. At the request of the client, the Dutch Ministry of Justice, the analysis was done in a short timeframe and with limited resources; hence the phrase 'quick scan' in the title of the report.

The quick scan covers a qualitative description of the initial reaction of the selected countries to the 9/11 events, characteristics of their national institutional framework regarding the fight against terrorism, and selected elements of their specific counter-terrorism policies and policy implementations. These descriptions are based on desk research and brief interviews with government officials. An analytic framework was designed to guide the approach and the analysis as well as to put the results in perspective.

The quick scan should be regarded as 'proof of concept'. For definitive analysis and comprehensive filling-out of the analytic framework, additional research is needed.

Summary

The initial post 9/11 reactions of the selected countries show no significant differences among the countries analysed. Top ministerial steering committees and task forces were quickly put together in all countries to provide leadership and a focal point in the confusion that followed the attacks. In particular the security and surveillance of commercial aviation, designated objects and components of critical infrastructures, dignitaries and, to a lesser extent, country borders were immediately strengthened. Intelligence gathering and intelligence sharing were increased, both domestically and internationally. All countries engaged in and adhered to international negotiations, most notably within the EU, but also with the UN, the USA and NATO, except Finland, which is not a NATO member. In fact, it might be inferred that the international coordination has created a productive atmosphere of harmonising countries' initial responses to the attacks. This is an important observation, bearing in mind that in the European Union, security is the sovereign responsibility of individual Member States.

In line with international resolutions, all countries have particularly stepped up their investment in the prevention of terrorism by increasing the capacity of intelligence, increasing the capacity to prevent money laundering, and strengthening the legal and law enforcement structure to deter terrorism and to bring terrorists to justice quickly, with increasing European harmonisation regarding the penal code. The rapid realisation of the European arrest warrant is a case in point. The point can be made however that it is too early to show the effects of such investments.

Differences among countries largely stem from previous national experiences with domestic terrorism and the (often associated) national institutional structures. Spain, The UK, France and Germany have more significant and more recent experience with domestic terrorism than Belgium and The Netherlands, and the experience of Finland in this respect could be classified as negligible. Some countries (Spain, France, Belgium, Germany and Finland) have a federal police chief or local police chiefs in large part in charge of preparing for or responding to terrorism. In other countries (Belgium and The Netherlands) the responsibility is shared among many government agencies and local agencies, although in principle it is still possible to identify lead institutions at the local and national level. Some countries (Spain, The UK, France and Germany) have specific laws on terrorism or have at least defined terrorism in their criminal code. Other countries (The Netherlands, Belgium and Finland) rely on criminal code to crack down on terrorists without a specific definition, building on the principle that every terrorist action will also be punishable by criminal law. However, that means that in these countries membership in terrorist organisations as such is not illegal and therefore not punishable. Since also the associated punishment in criminal code is more tolerant than in 'terrorist' code, the countries in question (Belgium, The Netherlands and Finland) may be

perceived by terrorists as safer heavens than other countries. This situation is recognised by the countries in question and will presumably be addressed in the near future.
None of the analysed countries specifically track government spending on counter-terrorism[1]. As a result, it is difficult to compare or analyse expenditures. On the other hand, most countries have identified the need to create budgets for additional counter-terrorism following 9/11. Mostly, these budgets are created through savings in other areas. Germany, on the other hand, has increased the tax levy on cigarettes and increased insurance taxes to obtain the budget resources. Increased aviation security is partly being paid for by a levy on airline tickets in all countries. From the limited data that we collected in this quick scan, we conclude that counter-terrorism expenditures in France, Germany, The UK and Spain are higher than in The Netherlands, Belgium and Finland; the same is true when normalised on a per capita basis.

None of the countries have a centralized national body to organise and orchestrate counter-terrorism, although France is moving towards it. By and large, their institutional frameworks consist of many players with well-defined partial responsibilities and partial authorities, plus coordinating bodies to make sure that information is shared timely and that rapid decision-making is facilitated. As terrorist attacks, according to all national perspectives on counter-terrorism, always strike locally, the first response will therefore also have to be local. Therefore, the authority for local response is clearly identified, although positions may differ between countries as to who actually has the authority (Chief Constable (THE UK), Mayor (The Netherlands) or Prefect (France), as examples). Also, the events of 9/11 have not generally changed countries' visions regarding the national institutional framework, including the role of the military. All countries have the impression that their existing framework and their existing capabilities plus the alterations and additions that were made post 9/11, are well matched with the perceived threat. Capabilities in most countries however are not matched with actual vulnerability, it seems[2]. All countries rate the likelihood of a domestic attack lower than is indicated by the events of 9/11, or earlier attempts that have been prevented by intelligence. Also, based on our interviews and various media reports, the level of urgency six months after 9/11, seems remarkably lower than immediately following the attacks. This could lead to the conclusion that at least additional training based on scenarios of terrorist attacks should test whether countries are well prepared in actuality.

The transparency of post 9/11 counter-terrorism policymaking varied among countries. In The Netherlands, a counter-terrorism action plan was quickly put together and continuously communicated with Congress, the media and the public at large, even on the Internet. The

---

[1] As opposed to for instance the USA, where the General Accounting Office (GAO) and the Office of Management and Budget (OMB) track counter-terrorism spending

[2] There is an interesting debate whether capabilities should primarily be established on the basis of vulnerabilities, or on a priority ranking of risks that follow from vulnerabilities and threats. Many analysts at RAND strongly adhere to the latter approach. In any case, systematic threat analyses and vulnerability analyses (e.g., risk analysis) often do not form the basis of counter-terrorism measures.

plan was subsequently updated every few months. The plan includes budgets and responsible actors and is still evolving. Other countries had less transparent policymaking processes, or if they had, they were discontinued within a period of 6 months following the attacks. Belgium did not inform the public very well. Nevertheless, most other countries made sure that the reactions were communicated in some form, albeit not as openly and detailed as The Netherlands.

In all countries, coordination between relevant authorities and agencies has increased, although it proved difficult to verify this independently. In the future, this increase may attribute to improved levels of prevention and preparedness. However, some interviewees indicated that effective coordination depends to a great extent on the sense of urgency and that improved coordination in itself is not always the key to prevention and preparedness. As an example, intelligence sharing in practice has been proven in the past to be resistant against the best theoretical intentions.

With respect to preparedness for attacks with non-conventional 'weapons of mass destruction', nuclear, biological, chemical, radiological weapons as well as and informational or 'cyber' weapons (collectively 'NBCRI'), we have the impression that all countries rate the associated threat low, in any case much lower than the threat of attacks with conventional weapons. Nevertheless, countries have taken some precautionary measures in the realm of NBCRI terrorist threats, ranging from only formal arrangements with national military R&D research and response units (Finland), to actually stocking up on vaccines, antibiotics and prophylaxes and outfitting local responders with decontamination units and personal protective gear (The Netherlands, France, Germany, The UK). Also, measures are being taken to improve the early detection of non-conventional weapons (Netherlands, France, THE UK, Germany, Spain), including both surface mobile and airborne units.

Although intelligence is generally considered to be paramount in countering terrorism, the nature of intelligence precludes in depth study of country characteristics, let alone comparison among countries. Associated with intelligence is the content and accessibility of databases related to counter-terrorism. Germany seems well advanced in data-mining[3] such databases ('Rasterfahndung'). This practice may lend itself to further international cooperation, but we should point out that although we are unaware of similar activities in other countries, such activities might well exist. Also, it is a sensitive issue, that call for careful approach. In a related issue, The Netherlands and Germany have suggested ways to improve biometrics in the future and focus currently on the quality and accessibility of fingerprint databases and the link with visas. We must however again emphasize that most data regarding intelligence in

[3] Data-mining is the ability to discover knowledge (in this case intelligence) from advanced search technology directed at (combinations of) databases.

general and this issue in particular is confidential and that therefore further and dedicated research is called for.

Although not part of the survey of the quick scan, we may observe that some countries' infrastructures are more vulnerable to attacks than others[4]. In particular, those countries' economies that rely heavily on large volumes of throughput of goods, persons and certain intangibles such as money, data and electricity, have associated interdependent critical networks and network nodes that make them vulnerable to terrorist attacks. The Netherlands and Belgium are such countries. It is therefore understandable that The Netherlands' next agenda item in counter-terrorism is critical infrastructure protection and that it is expected to become a major issue on the national security agenda. One particular aspect that seems not to have received balanced and worldwide security attention yet is container transport -- certainly not in the countries we surveyed. This issue may be of relatively high relevance to small countries with large harbours, such as Belgium and The Netherlands, although of course all other surveyed countries have important harbours that could be attacked.

Although all countries, including non-NATO member Finland, offered and delivered support to the military component of the international fight against the Al Queda network, The UK, France and Germany were actually and most significantly involved in aerial and ground combat in Afghanistan. (An in-depth assessment of military operational responses to and preparedness in light of 9/11 however was not performed).

The conclusions in this report are not definitive or comprehensive. That, after all, comes with the nature of a quick scan. However, this report can be regarded as indicative of potentially important differences and commonalities. We therefore recommend that any specific issues that arise should be researched further before determining any specific action.

The Table on the next page summarises the result of this quick scan. It provides a colour-coded matrix of progress that countries have made with respect to measures in certain areas of counter-terrorism. The counter-terrorism areas follow the descriptions identified in the results of the quick scan. It should be emphasised that the colour codes are not definitive in any way, both as a result of the limited nature of the quick scan as well as of the dynamic nature of domestic post 9/11 counter-terrorism policymaking.

---

[4] See also www.ddsi.org

Broad area of counter-terrorism measures	Finland	France	Germany	Nether-lands	Spain	United Kingdom
Top level responsibility assigned						
Protect potential targets						
Aviation security						
Increased intelligence						
Act upon & create lists of suspects						
International cooperation						
Financial surveillance & intervention						
Institutional change						
Legal harmonisation						
NBCRI preparedness						
Cybersecurity						
Infrastructure protection						
Increase policy transparency						
Identify levels of domestic vigilance						
Military action abroad						
Biometrics Data / visa						
Private sector involvement						

Color coding	No specific post 9/11 measures needed	Need identified, no action	Some action	Well underway	Accom-plished

Legend:

Top level responsibility assigned — Set up of top level committees and task forces directly following 9/11
Protect potential targets — Protecting embassies, bridges, tunnels, dignitaries
Aviation security — Implementing 100% luggage and passenger checks – all flights
Increased intelligence — Increase capacity for cooperation and coordination
Act upon & create lists of suspects — Seize and identify suspects linked with terrorism
International cooperation — Contribute actively in international bodies for CT policymaking
Financial surveillance & intervention — Freeze assets, monitor money flows and transactions
Institutional change — Change institutional domestic framework regarding CT prevention and response
Legal harmonisation — Harmonise penal code and identify terrorism in legal code
NBCRI preparedness — Monitoring, prevention, decontamination prophylaxis regarding various WMD
Cyber-security — Implement strategic measures in protection against cyber terrorists
Infrastructure protection — Come up with integrated plans for critical infrastructure protection
Increase policy transparency — Detailed information of public at large, interdepartmental, inter-institutional
Identify levels of domestic vigilance — identify levels of domestic vigilance linked to increased activity of all stakeholders
Military action abroad — Participate in active military operations and combat
Biometrics data/visa — Create database and realise access regarding visa
Private sector involvement — Seek clear role and commitment from private sector; sense of urgency

Table of Contents

Section 1: Main report

Introduction

Background

The terrorist attacks of 11 September 2001 have shown dramatically that the 'new terrorism' is different from the old[5]. It is global, it is decentralised, it uses new strategies and tactics, and it is increasingly focused upon building the capacity for mass casualty and mass destruction attacks, in an effort to destabilise entire societal systems. Attacks could entail the use of any imaginable weapon: conventional, chemical, biological, nuclear, radiological and informational – individually or in combination. Consequently, it threatens all sectors and infrastructures of society. Increasingly, terrorists are loosely organised in networked structures. Europe's democratic, open societies, its globalised transportation systems, its concentrated cities, its highly developed infrastructures and its permeable borders provide a harbour, access routes and targets to the new networked terrorists. The fact that Europe is an outspoken member of the coalition against terrorism puts Europe on the front-line of the campaign against terrorism, and potentially increases its profile as a target. An attack on Europe or Europe's allies may well be planned and prepared with European resources and infrastructures.

In reality, directly following the tragic events of 11 September 2001, many governments, including European governments, rapidly reviewed anti- and counter-terrorism[6] capabilities and terrorism-preparedness on a national basis, giving priority to domestic policies and measures and looking at strengths and weaknesses within their own borders. Supranational and international guidance was provided by the European Union's Justice and Home Affairs Council and by UN as well as by NATO. By and large, however, governments were so busy in the first months after the attacks formulating and implementing counter-terrorism policies that there was not enough time to coordinate internationally these policies at all levels of detail. But now that the national responses to 9/11 are entering the implementation phase, the question arises whether nations worldwide and European Member States in particular, should take further steps with regard to coordination and cooperation regarding the fight against terrorism. This is the background against which the Dutch Ministry of Justice asked RAND Europe to conduct a quick scan of post 9/11 national counter-terrorism policymaking and policy implementation of selected European Member States.

---

[5] 'The new terrorism has different motives, different actors, different sponsors and … demonstrably greater lethality. Terrorists are also organising themselves in new, les hierarchical structures and making use of amateurs to a far greater extent than in the past. All of this renders much previous analysis of terrorism … obsolete, and complicates the task of intelligence gathering and counterterrorism. In: Lesser, I.O., Bruce Hoffman, John Arquila, David Ronfeldt and Michele Zanini (1999) Countering the New Terrorism. RAND, Santa Monica.

[6] Anti-terrorism comprises defensive measures in the fight against terrorism. Counter-terrorism describes offensive measures. Preparedness is the capability to respond to terrorist threats and attacks. In the remainder of this report we will use the term counter-terrorism to cover both anti – and counter-terrorism.

Problem definition

Since 9/11, governments worldwide have worked hard to update their national agenda's for the improvement of capabilities to fight terrorism and to initiate the implementation of such updates at the shortest possible notice. While doing this, they have generally tried to operate against the background of perceived threats and existing national strengths and weaknesses. For instance, as a large percentage of The Netherlands' surface area is below sea level, the vulnerability to flooding is a specific Dutch weakness that required extra attention. Therefore, it was considered necessary to pay extra attention to the dependability of water management systems. On the other hand, a specific strength of The Netherlands regarding the fight against terrorism is the capability to monitor financial flows in detail. The Dutch banking system is quite transparent. This element therefore required no drastic extra measures. Comparable aspects may be different in other countries. In other words, policymaking and implementation in one country may differ largely from another depending on specific national characteristics. But it may also differ as a result of other factors, such as perceived urgency, available budgets, and the intricacies of each country's national security system, including the division of responsibilities and authority between government institutions and the focus on prevention versus preparedness and response.

In light of the above, the Dutch Ministry of Justice, which carried the responsibility of operational oversight of the Dutch government's response to the 11 September attacks, became interested in rapidly gaining more insight into these differences in order to get a comparative impression of the characteristics and appropriateness of its own policymaking and implementation. This is one major consideration in support of the quick scan that this report describes.

A chain is as strong as the weakest link. For instance, failing airplane security procedures in one country affect the security of another country. Thus, global security depends on the complex interdependence of the myriad of national measures at all levels. To know the strengths and weaknesses of the counter-terrorism policies and policy implementations of allies or at least of neighbouring countries would therefore provide useful insight into the overall situation regarding the fight against terrorism. As this aspect has so far not received adequate attention in considering a national agenda to combat terrorism, there is now some urgency to consider other countries' positions. This is a second consideration in support of this quick scan.

Combining these two considerations, there is a double need to know more about other countries' policymaking and policy implementation for combating terrorism after 11 September 2001. As threat analysis shows that critical infrastructures (such as surface transport and aviation, energy, financial and communication systems as well as health and food systems) of modern societies are most vulnerable to 'new terrorist' attacks, and as the

Dutch Ministry of Justice perceives a certain level of urgency, it seemed wise to start quickly to gain insight into other countries' capabilities by looking specifically at selected neighbouring countries. After all, these neighbouring countries most often share or use parts of common infrastructures, such as transportation. For broader comparison however, some non-neighbouring countries were included in the analysis as well. Of course, since the problem is global, only an analysis of all countries of the world would provide the total coverage needed. However, such an approach would not be practical at this point.

These considerations can be summarized into the following problem definition for this quick scan:

What national policy initiatives were taken after 11 September 2001 to prevent and respond to future terrorist attacks and how were these initiatives implemented in selected Member States of the European Union? How do these policies and implementations compare with the ones in The Netherlands?

Approach

Country selection

Choosing the 'neighbouring' countries of The Netherlands was self-evident.

- Germany
- Belgium
- France
- The United Kingdom

In relative terms, Belgium is a smaller country, economically, politically and militarily, than the others. France and the UK are of course not neighbours in the purely geographical sense, but are considered such for all practical purposes.

For broader comparison, we chose to include only a couple of non-neighbouring countries as more would negatively affect the speed with which this quick scan could be executed. Needless to say, including all member states of the European Union, or other relevant countries, such as the USA, would have provided a better overview on one hand, but would have demanded much more resources on the other hand. We therefore choose as the non-neighbours the following two countries:

- Finland
- Spain

Finland is known to have had relatively little experience with terrorism, whereas Spain is known to having been continuously exposed to terrorism. Therefore, these two non-neighbouring countries were expected to significantly add to the comparative spectrum while keeping the total number of countries low.

Research team

We put together a research team consisting of six researchers, plus two advisors. The researchers were selected so that interviews could be held with country authorities in their native language and against the background of shared knowledge of national systems and culture. The advisors are both highly regarded for their general knowledge about security and specific knowledge about combating terrorism. In accordance with RAND Europe policy, the quick scan underwent an independent quality assessment.

Authors

Erik J.G. van de Linde, Project Leader, Rand Europe, Leiden, The Netherlands

Stephan De Spiegeleire, RAND Europe, Leiden, The Netherlands

Han de Vries, RAND Europe, Leiden, The Netherlands

Kevin O'Brien, RAND Europe, Cambridge, THE UK

Gustav Lindstrom, RAND Graduate School, Santa Monica, California, USA

Mikko Vayrynen, FIIA, Finnish Institute of International Affairs, Helsinki, Finland

Advisors

David Gompert, President, RAND Europe, Leiden, The Netherlands

Ian Lesser, Terrorism Expert, RAND, Washington, DC, USA

Quality Assessment

Michael Wermuth, Terrorism Expert, RAND, Washington, DC, USA

Initial desk research

Individual researchers were assigned to a country to collect preliminary data. Mostly, government websites were used for this purpose, in some cases supplemented with short phone calls to appropriate authorities. This preliminary information was then compared to make a decision about the analytic framework to be applied for this study.

Analytic framework

A common reference framework is essential. While this is generally true for all research and analysis, it is especially true in the case of comparative analysis, and even more strongly so in highly complex cases where many factors are interdependent. Counter-terrorism is such a case. But not only will a solid analytic framework provide a necessary tool for this particular study, it will also provide perspective and overview regarding the complex area of counter-terrorism in general. As such, the analytic framework may also be regarded as a useful result of this study that can be applied in other future counter-terrorism analysis. As we are unaware of other analytic frameworks for comparative analyses in the area of counter-terrorism, we hope to provide a first step to fill that gap.

After having decided on the analytic framework, the team members set out to collect data more systematically, among others by approaching a small number of government officials with detailed questions.

The framework that we have constructed for this study consists of four major dimensions:

- Challenges
- Measures
- Actors
- Stage

All four dimensions consist of several sub-dimensions that we will describe down to a relevant and useful level of detail. But first we will briefly discuss the four major dimensions.

Dimension 1: Challenges

'Challenges' are the issues that countries need to address to prevent, deter, respond to, mitigate and recover from terrorist threats or terrorist attacks effectively. These threats and attacks may be hypothetical or real. They may have occurred in the past, they may play in the present or they may play in the future. What a challenge is precisely depends largely on the nature of the threat or the nature of the attack. Threat and attack can be seen as a combination of (potential) weapons and (potential) targets. Weapons can be conventional, non-conventional, including both weapons of mass destruction (WMD) and non-WMD; and targets can range from individual human beings (important dignitaries and VIPs, but also ordinary citizens) to large numbers of people, critical infrastructures, as well as other targets. The essence is that challenges are the reasons why countries have to engage in counter-terrorism.

Dimension 2: Measures

This second dimension is in fact a compilation of all necessary responses to challenges. Sub-dimensions are categories of responses. Main categories are strategic, operational and tactical. Examples of categories of measures are planning, training, exercising, equipping, raising awareness, monitoring money transfers, information sharing, stockpiling of antibiotics, outfitting first responders, law enforcement cooperation, etc. These may be detailed further, down to the level of individual measures, for instance personal protection of ambulance personnel against biological or chemical agents, or monitoring the contents of shipping containers by way of x-ray. In fact, we did some of that detailing in this project, focusing on post 9/11 measures. This will be explained extensively in a later section of this chapter.

Dimension 3: Actors

The third dimension deals with the question of who is responsible for implementing the measures for responding to a particular challenge. Examples of sub-dimensions are federal, state and local; civil and military; public and private. Of course these again can be further detailed, ranging from the chief of the local fire brigade, for example, to the Minister of Internal Affairs, and we will do so later. For now, it suffices to emphasize that this 'Actor' dimension deals with assigning responsibility with regard to measures and challenges.

Of course certain actors will be responsible for certain measures that correspond with certain challenges. This is how the three dimensions are interdependent. Also, one actor may be responsible for many measures (for instance, the Chief of Federal Police may have the overall policymaking responsibility for response during an attack), and one challenge may call for many measures of many actors. This is why counter-terrorism is complex: many actors and many interdependencies.

Dimension 4: Stage

The first three dimensions -- Challenges, Measures and Actors -- together form a three-dimensional space (i.e., a cube) representing the counter-terrorism area. We will position these first three dimensions relative to time, or the 'stage' of an actual threat or attack. The sub-dimensions within the 'Stage' dimension are pre-, trans- and post-attack. In pre-attack, pre-emption is important, consisting of preparation, prevention, protection and deterrence. During an attack, and immediately following it ('trans'), response including detection and interdiction and mitigation are important. Post attack, important sub-dimensions are recovery, counter-attack and implementation of lessons learned in the counter-terrorism cycle.

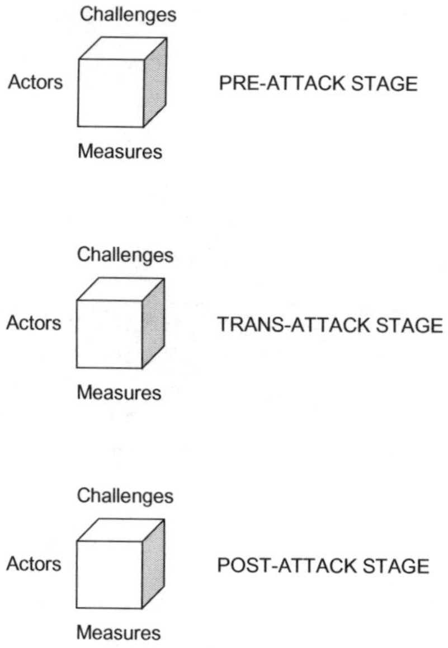

Fig 1. Overview of the analytic framework with the four major dimensions Challenge, Measures, Actors, and Stage

Applying the analytic framework in this quick scan

One way to analyse counter-terrorism policies and their implementation would be to systematically check all the cells[7] of the framework at a particular level of sub-dimension detail. In each cell, we could research what measures have been assigned to what actors, responding to which challenges, relative to what stage. Clearly, even if only three sub-dimensions were used in an approach like this, and if this approach were applied to a number of countries, already a large study would result. However, with only three sub-dimensions per dimensions, not enough detail would be provided in this approach to come up with meaningful results, again indicating that such an approach would quickly result in a massive study. Therefore, in this quick scan, we will use the analytic framework from the opposite direction. We will first identify individual items of post 9/11 counter-terrorism policymaking and

[7] A 'cell' is a space defined by Challenge (x), Measures (y), Actor(z) and Stage(w)

implementation and then classify them according to the analytic framework. Using the analytic framework in this way corresponds with the nature of a quick scan.

First we identify individual items of post 9/11 counter-terrorism policymaking and implementation and then classify them according to the analytic framework.

Surely, this approach will leave many of the cells of the analytic framework blank. After all, the framework is broad, and can cover 'old' and 'new' terrorism and both pre- and post 9/11 policymaking and implementation, while in the quick scan we are only narrowly focusing on post 9/11. Of course that does not mean that there are no measures to be recognized at all in blank cells. On the contrary; we can generally assume that post 9/11 counter-terrorism action plans are formulated such that they cover the highest priorities (considering all dimensions of the analytic framework) per country. Post 9/11 measures are either meant to respond to new challenges of the New Terrorism, or - to a lesser extent - to fill gaps in the terrorism preparedness that were already there in light of the pre 9/11 perspective. In line with this assumption, we can postulate that 'cells' in the analytic framework that are not covered apparently do not need special action right now for various reasons. But there is also a possibility that a certain challenge has been overlooked. Therefore, the three most important considerations regarding empty cells are:

- The challenge has such a high priority that it had already been taken care of before 9/11
- The challenge has a low priority (because it represents a low risk or is perceived as such) and thus requires no further immediate action
- The challenge has been overlooked and may represent a serious risk.

Again, this quick scan doesn't allow checking why blank cells of the analytic framework remain empty. The resources of the quick scan were too limited; that comprehensive, systematic analysis will have to be postponed to follow-up work. This quick scan may however be looked at as 'proof of concept'. In other words, we are looking for data and experience that may provide support to the concept of comparing counter-terrorism policies on the basis of the framework used here.

In the future, we could for instance try to identify three different cross-country categories of cells:

- Cells that are covered by all countries
- Cells that are not covered by any country
- Cells that are covered by some countries

The last category may provide an interesting opportunity for targeted future analysis as to why, apparently, some challenges and measures are assigned a high priority in some countries, but a low priority in others.

Sub-dimensions

In the following we provide further detail of the four dimensions in as far we think that this detail may be necessary to allow for meaningful results on one hand, while staying within the limits of the quick scan on the other hand.

Challenges

Challenges consist of the combination of weapons and targets[8]. It has been recognized that the *New Terrorism* strives to inflict mass casualties of ordinary civilians and mass destruction of critical infrastructures while using unconventional weapons, such as WMD[9]. But the 'new terrorism' does not preclude the 'old', which uses conventional weapons and targets individual dignitaries and VIP's (attacking politicians, businessmen, athletes). Therefore, our reference framework for the dimension 'Challenges' could look like this:

Weapon	Conventional[10]	WMD (NBCRI)
Target		
Individuals	1	2
Mass casualty	3	4
Infrastructures	5	6

This matrix provides six major sub-dimensions. Examples of challenges for each of these could be:

1. Killing a government official with a grenade
2. Threatening a businessman with anthrax
3. Levelling a heavily populated office building with a truck bomb
4. Chemical attack on a population concentration (e.g., major sporting event) with a lethal persistent nerve agent
5. Blowing a gas pipeline
6. Cyber attack on financial data networks (or radiological 'dirty bomb' in a major seaport)

---

[8] Of course, risk is a major factor here as well. Risk is the product of likelihood (threat plus vulnerability) and impact. Low probability, high impact challenges may have the same level of comparative risk as high probability, low impact. Risk analysis is not part of this quick scan. However, national governments do take risk into account when they put together their national action plans, either explicitly or implicitly

[9] A common classification of WMD is: Nuclear, Biological, Chemical, Radiological and Informational. Whether the latter category can be seen as mass destructive is debatable

[10] Guns and explosives

Of course, some weapons may be regarded as mass destructive and conventional as well, such in the case of 9/11. Also, some 'weapons' may be targeting combinations of targets. One could therefore argue that separate categories are needed for these. However, for all practical purposes, we believe that these six sub-dimensions cover the challenges that require consideration in this study. Finally we recognize that many policies are not targeted at any specific single challenge. Intelligence, for instance, would cover all possible challenges. In cases where policies do not discriminate between challenges, we have indicated a '0' in the associated cells in the framework matrix.

Measures

We do not believe that a further sub-dimensioning than the method outlined earlier, i.e. strategic, operational and tactical is necessary for our purposes.

Strategic measures would be long-term measures preparing for certain challenges. Examples of this would be to change the organisational structure of the national security system or to develop national plans for combating terrorism.

Operational measures would include freezing financial assets of known or suspected terrorist organisations or their financiers, or implementing and enforcing sanctions against a country that provide support to terrorists.

Tactical measures could be to set up local crisis management plans, or to provide improved equipment to response organisations.

Actors

To break down the dimension of actors, we will have to consider federal, state and local; public and private; as well as military and non-military. A sub-matrix is not needed here however, since the military is only a central actor, and the private sector is only a local actor. Therefore, the breakdown looks like this:

- Public sector, federal/national level, civil (including special forces)
- Public sector, regional/state level, civil
- Public sector, local level, civil
- Military
- Private sector (all levels)

This results in five sub-dimensions. Again, there may be borderline cases that call for judgment or even a separate subdimension, such as the Special Forces in some countries, that are part of the military in terms of training and equipment, but non-military in terms of command structure. However, we believe that the five sub-dimensions above will suffice.

With the three sub-dimensions for 'Stage', the analytic framework looks like:

Challenges (6) x Measures (3) x Actors (5) x Stage (3) = 270 cells

Validation of data in the analytic framework

Once we categorised measures in the 270-cell framework based on desk research, we interviewed several key persons per country to validate that categorization. In addition, we asked interviewees to provide us with additional measures that we had overlooked, as well as with additional data per measure, such as implementation stage, budget, etc. Thus, for post-9/11 measures, we could code measures in terms of state of progress as follows:

1. No specific post 9/11 action
2. Need for action identified, policy in the making
3. Budget appropriated, actors identified
4. Policy implementation well underway
5. Policy implementation finalised

In the interview, we provided the opportunity to interviewees to comment on why certain 'cells' were not covered in the action plan as they saw fit to do so. However, we did not systematically ask this question for all cells, as the limitations on the quick scan did not allow for it. Also, the function of the quick scan, we foresaw, would be to point out that certain cells could remain irrelevant for practical purposes, while other could turn out to be important but requiring more detailed research.

More specifically, the following issues were discussed in the interviews:

- Is the categorisation correct?
- In what state of progress is the measure (1-5)?
- Are there any post 9/11 measures we have missed? (Most notably late additions to road maps)
- Are there any particular aspects of the measures that should be highlighted? (For instance 'high priority', or 'international cooperation crucial')
- Are there certain empty 'cells' that you want to comment on?

Limitations

The quick scan has a wide scope, but as a consequence the level of detail is limited. We were unable to systematically check all relevant issues with interviewees. Also we were able to interview just a few key persons. Many key persons were difficult to reach and the extent to which reports and data are available was often limited, due both to the often-confidential nature of the subject and its ‘in progress’ status. Also, counter-terrorism policies are constantly evolving and changing. The analysis based on our findings must therefore be regarded as preliminary – a ‘snapshot’ in time, in other words – and all relevant issues must be researched in further detail before any conclusions can be cast in stone. One function of this quick scan may therefore be to set a more detailed research agenda. As such, the quick scan should be looked at in terms of 'proof of concept'.

Results

We believe that the approach in this quick scan holds promise for a more detailed and comprehensive analysis. The analytic framework employed here allows for useful categorisation of counter-terrorism policies, but the study lacked the necessary resources, as expected, to apply the framework to a level of detail necessary to draw sharp conclusions and to identify many clear distinctions between countries.

In order to make a useful quantitative comparison, we would suggest performing additional research, focussing in more detail on the following areas where preventive counter-terrorism measures have been taken or considered by all countries in one way or another, in order of priority:

- Intelligence
- Finance
- Legal
- Military
- NBCRI
- Critical infrastructures
- Research and development
- Institutional framework

This quick scan however does offer a qualitative description of post 9/11 counter-terrorism policymaking and policy implementation in seven selected European member states. We catalogued a number of commonalities in their reactions. There is no doubt that this is the result of coordination that took place within international bodies such as the European Union, the United Nations, the international coalition against terrorism led by the USA, and, to a lesser extent, NATO.

Differences between countries are relatively few and seem mostly rooted in the context of experience with domestic terrorism in the recent past as well as in the characteristics of the national institutional framework regarding counter-terrorism responsibility and authority.

The initial sense of urgency that was apparent in all countries following the 9/11 attacks has materialised in extensive actions and initiatives, largely aimed at prevention through protection of critical objects, increased intelligence, strengthening the legal structure and cracking down on money laundering. Although all countries engaged in some military aspect of the fight against terrorism, and some countries prepared for or even engaged in actual combat (e.g., UK and France), the conclusion is justified that, in general, the European answer (of the seven countries studied) to international terrorism is neither to strengthen the military significantly nor to change its mission materially.

In our discussions and observations, we noticed that the initial sense of urgency following the attacks of 9/11 has largely dissipated. This is due, in some measure, to the fact that high-level (steering committee) policymaking is now being implemented. Also, many European governments have a general policy refraining from issuing unspecified warnings and statements.

All seven countries have exhibited common reactions to the events of 9/11. First of all, they have swiftly put together Ministerial steering committees that took charge of measures necessary to counter the actual or perceived challenges. These committees provided leadership and a focal point for the public, the media and all those involved in counter-terrorism at the national, provincial and the local levels. In order of priority, these committees oversaw the initiation of the following actions in all countries:

- Setting up a top level response structure (committee, task forces)
- Protecting potential targets (power plants, bridges, tunnels, waterways, borders, food & water, embassies, foreign companies)
- Increasing airport and aviation security (persons, luggage, aircraft)
- Stepping up intelligence and information sharing (Civil, Military, Europol, International, threat analysis)
- Engaging in international consultation (European Union, USA, NATO) and adhering to resolutions where appropriate
- Act upon and assist in developing international lists of terrorists or terrorist organisations
- Following financial leads to terrorists and freezing assets (using various lists)
- Adopting international counter terrorist resolutions at increased pace (mostly UN)
- Re-evaluating institutional frameworks for responsibility and authority (None of the countries have centralised organisations specifically aimed at terrorism. No significant changes were deemed necessary and the important role of first responders was recognized)
- Harmonising legislation (for instance the European Arrest Warrant[11])
- Increasing preparedness for WMD (monitoring, diagnosis, prophylaxis)
- Understanding aspects of the *New Terrorism* (in particular biological and chemical weapons)
- Initiating R&D initiatives for increasing dependability of critical infrastructures

---

[11] European Union (EU) member states' judiciary will no longer have to go through the formal extradition procedure in order to forcibly transfer a person from one member state to another for conducting a criminal prosecution or executing a custodial sentence or detention order. On 11 December 2001, the EU reached a political agreement on the European arrest warrant. Its purpose is to facilitate law enforcement right across the EU. (Europa.eu.int/comm/justice_home/news/laecken_council/en/mandat_en.htm)

While all seven countries exhibited similar approaches to 9/11 initially, there were differences in how responsive actions were carried out and how they evolved.

- Although all countries set up ministerial committees and top-level governmental task forces, these have been dissolved already in some countries (e.g., Finland and Belgium).
- Some governments kept a rather accessible paper trail of their activities, in order to share the progress with the general public, the media and congress. Germany has published two counter-terrorism legislative packages and communicated these extensively with all relevant stakeholders, including the public at large. The Netherlands has published a list of actions, which is continuously updated, together with associated budgets, responsibilities and sometimes suggestions for further action, on the websites of relevant departments. The Council of the European Union also has published very openly its resolutions, approaches and 'roadmaps' accordingly[12] on the web, but although the other six countries that were studied certainly kept minutes of their progress, they were not put together in an openly published form. Some countries (like Belgium) regard their action plans as confidential, and the inventory of national responses that was drawn up by Europol is equally not public.
- The protection of critical objects in some countries has already returned to less high levels (e.g., The Netherlands, Finland and Belgium) whereas other countries have maintained their level of vigilance (e.g. France, Spain and UK). It seems that those countries that had significant experience with domestic terrorism are more likely to extend stepped-up levels of security for a longer period.
- Some countries can declare certain levels of increased alert in counter-terrorism, most notably France. This is an area that could maybe be harmonised throughout Europe.
- All countries have increased their intelligence collection, analysis, dissemination and coordination, but some countries have dedicated much more capacity to do so (e.g., France) than others. Also, the authority for intelligence agencies to operate seems broader in some countries, notably France, Spain and Germany. Also, in countries that seem to have rather autonomous intelligence units, the ties between military and civil intelligence seems strongest. This seems to occur in countries whose police force is organised federally (France, Spain, and Belgium) as opposed to locally (The Netherlands, Finland, The UK and Germany).
- In the international arena, the dedication to military action, and in particular in supporting Operation Enduring Freedom, has been very apparent but has also been very different between countries. Here, The UK is clearly in the lead, followed by

[12] see for instance the EU counter-terrorism roadmap of 9 april 2002 on http://register.consilium.eu.int/pdf/en/02/st07/07686en2.pdf

France. All countries however have provided some support albeit not in actual air or ground combat, even Finland, although it is not a member of NATO.

- Some countries cracked down hard on terrorists whose names appeared on international lists of suspects (name on these lists often were provided through US intelligence in connection with Operation Enduring Freedom). In particular in Germany, France, The UK, and Spain, several terrorists were captured and brought before court.
- All countries obtained lists of organisations suspected of financing terrorism, and subsequently engaged in various initiatives to freeze their assets. In some countries (France and Germany) this resulted in the blocking of a large number of accounts and assets, but in others (Belgium and The Netherlands) eventually no assets were blocked.
- Institutional national frameworks for structuring the responsibility and authority for counter-terrorism differ with respect to the role of the military and the role of the police. It seems that those countries that recognise terrorism in their legislation and that have a federal police (France, Spain) exhibit a much stronger role for police, than countries that do not. The Netherlands for instance shows a lead role for the Ministry of Justice and Internal Affairs and a supporting role for other Ministries, including Defence. This is in contrast with some other countries in which the role of the military is more pronounced (France, Spain).
- Finland and The Netherlands both do not recognise terrorism in the penal code. Therefore, the penalty for terrorist activities is milder than in other countries. This situation will likely be corrected and harmonised in the coming years[13].
- The Netherlands, Germany and Spain have emphasized the use of biometrics databases, initially focussing on fingerprints only, to keep better track of migration, in particular of refugees that often lack passports or other identity papers.
- In reality, governments' threat assessment of the *New Terrorism* indicates that classical terrorism (conventional weapons, individual targets) is more likely to happen than the *New Terrorism* that may use weapons of mass destruction (NBCRI) and attacks infrastructures. Therefore the risk associated with classical terrorism is still considered to be largest. Nevertheless, most countries have engaged in particular activities to strengthen the knowledge about biological and chemical weapons, to stockpile vaccines and antibiotics and to train and equip first responders accordingly. France has a standing 'biotox' plan that already addressed the issue. The Netherlands is particularly engaged in producing smallpox vaccine and in improving diagnostic capability, but other countries as well, such as Belgium, Spain and even Finland have dedicated specific attention to aspects of WMD, most notably B, C and I. In many countries, the government often relies on NBC know-how that is present in

[13] Legislation has been drafted in The Netherlands that recognises membership of a criminal organisation with a terrorist goal. The draft is currently under consideration by the Council of State

the military -- Finland almost completely. The Netherlands has stepped up its R&D to increase the expert knowledge level. Spain, France and The UK have considerable experience in the field already. Germany has so far abstained from special actions in this field.

- Lastly, the issue of infrastructure dependability[14] has to do with the complex issue of 'domino' effects, where small failures in one infrastructure, may cause large ones in another and thus affect the intricate fabric of modern societies. Since many critical infrastructures are increasingly liberalised (finance, food, energy, transport, telecom, and to lesser extent water, security, health, education) protecting the interdependent infrastructures requires not just the collaboration of industry, but even a leading role for the private sector. Therefore, albeit important, this issue has so far been low on the priority list of countries. However, some countries, in particular The UK, Germany and The Netherlands have at least engaged in initial rounds of thinking and agenda setting.

Clearly, all countries' priorities are prevention through intelligence, cutting off terrorists' resources, increased surveillance and security and improving the legal structure. To be able to do so, several agencies, departments and law enforcement units are being strengthened with personnel. This is the largest priority as well as a large difficulty, because often, not enough trained personnel are available. Equipment, mainly of an informational nature, such as easy and rapid access to visa databases, and diagnostic equipment, such as x-ray scanners to detect metal objects, offers less of a problem – again, it is the personnel required to work with the equipment that requires the largest investment.

Even although all countries have intensively engaged in international coordination, often through permanent representatives in the European Union and the UN, and embassy personnel and other staff normally engaged in international deliberations, there has been little time for national governments to actually explore directly in the first six months after the 9/11 attacks how events evolved in other member states, other than indirectly through Council meetings and the work of the UN Counter Terrorism Committee (CTC). This quick scan is of course one way to fill that gap.

Another gap is the involvement of the private sector. Of course, private sector security companies are involved in securing company buildings and even public infrastructure, but what is meant here is the responsibility of the private sector regarding issues such as dependability of critical infrastructures. Since these are increasingly socio-technical, the private sector should carry a responsibility in relation to personnel and systems. Those issues are being addressed necessarily in the aviation industry; in other areas, such as container

---

[14] See also www.ddsi.org

transport, the responsibility of the private sector has not been adequately addressed in any of the researched countries.

Again, most of the seven countries' threat assessment is such that the classical terrorism is still considered to pose a larger risk than the new terrorism. Consequently, protection against and prevention of attacks with WMD did not receive very significant extra attention. In particular, the threat of a nuclear attack is considered unlikely. However, all countries support international efforts in the area of non-proliferation of nuclear weapons. In general, countries seem confident about the match of their measures with the perceived threat, but when asked, the measures seem to match less well with specific vulnerabilities, such as in the transportation system or in energy networks.

European countries in general have had experience in the recent past with domestic terrorist attacks, or at least with terrorism in neighbouring countries. As a result, some systems are in place to deal with various terrorist threats and attacks, and, most importantly, to try to prevent them. Most countries are used to the requirement to coordinate among large numbers of entities that play a role, or they are at least willing to improve that coordination. As information sharing is probably the best weapon in the fight against terrorism, this puts European countries in a good starting position in the fight against terrorism. Also, the unification of Europe provides an additional atmosphere for information sharing.

Europe's strength is also its weakness. Its modern societies provide easy access to infrastructures. As a result, terrorist organisations are easily supported, but the same infrastructures could also be targets. On one hand, securing these infrastructures may be increasingly difficult as a result of the general socio-technical development, including market mechanisms and globalisation. On the other hand, these very mechanisms may cause increasing redundancy in infrastructures, and thereby decreasing vulnerability. This paradox will have to be addressed by European nations. Also, the current lack of centralised responsibility for security within the European Union may be regarded as a weakness. France in particular would like to change that situation in the future, by the establishment of a European police force.

Finally, an important supportive infrastructure for terrorism is formed by networks of international crime, often related to trafficking of drugs, humans, cars, illegal weapons and other contraband, and various kinds of fraud. According to a spokesman of Interpol, international crime is on the rise, particularly in The Netherlands, but also in some other countries outside this quick scan. This positions The Netherlands, together with its relatively tolerant penal code, open borders, large main ports, etc., as a country that may be favoured by international terrorist networks. Turning this argument around, we may say that fighting crime will help to fight terrorism as well.

The following table visualises the findings.

Broad area of counter-terrorism measures	Finland	France	Germany	Nether-lands	Spain	United Kingdom
Top level responsibility assigned						
Protect potential targets						
Aviation security						
Increased intelligence						
Act upon & create lists of suspects						
International cooperation						
Financial surveillance & intervention						
Institutional change						
Legal harmonisation						
NBCRI preparedness						
Cybersecurity						
Infrastructure protection						
Increase policy transparency						
Identify levels of domestic vigilance						
Military action abroad						
Biometrics Data / visa						
Private sector involvement						

Color coding	No specific post 9/11 measures needed	Need identified, no action	Some action	Well underway	Accom-plished

Legend:

Top level responsibility assigned	Set up of top level committees and task forces directly following 9/11
Protect potential targets	Protecting embassies, bridges, tunnels, dignitaries
Aviation security	Implementing 100% luggage and passenger checks – all flights
Increased intelligence	Increase capacity for cooperation and coordination
Act upon & create lists of suspects	Seize and identify suspects linked with terrorism
International cooperation	Contribute actively in international bodies for CT policymaking
Financial surveillance & intervention	Freeze assets, monitor money flows and transactions
Institutional change	Change institutional domestic framework regarding CT prevention and response
Legal harmonisation	Harmonise penal code and identify terrorism in legal code
NBCRI preparedness	Monitoring, prevention, decontamination prophylaxis regarding various WMD
Cyber-security	Implement strategic measures in protection against cyber terrorists
Infrastructure protection	Come up with integrated plans for critical infrastructure protection
Increase policy transparency	Detailed information of public at large, interdepartmental, inter-institutional
Identify levels of domestic vigilance	identify levels of domestic vigilance linked to increased activity of all stakeholders
Military action abroad	Participate in active military operations and combat
Biometrics data/visa	Create database and realise access regarding visa
Private sector involvement	Seek clear role and commitment from private sector; sense of urgency

Comparing The Netherlands to other countries

Keeping in mind the limitations in detail, depth and level of certainty inherent in a quick-scan, it is possible to make some preliminary observations regarding how The Netherlands compares to at least the other countries examined.

There are a number of areas in which The Netherlands appears to be at least as advanced as any of the other countries.

- Biometrics
- Use of advanced surveillance technologies and techniques
- Financial transaction monitoring and intervention
- Environmental damage assessment and remediation
- Bio/chem-terrorism prevention and response

This does not necessarily mean that the other countries are weak in these areas. In fact, all appear to have strengths in one or another. However, it might behoove The Netherlands to explore whether it might offer help in any of these areas to countries that might not be as far advanced, for whatever reason.

There are also some areas in which, according to our Quick Scan, other countries might have moved further and/or more quickly further than The Netherlands, among them:

- Finland appears to have made a major effort in countering cyber-terrorism. (This would be consistent with the high-priority Finland has placed on cyber-security for some time.)
- France has taken steps to bolster defense of its airspace. We did not discover in our Quick Scan what steps in this direction The Netherlands has taken.
- Although The Netherlands appears relatively advanced in bio/chem-terrorism response, it is not clear from the Quick Scan whether it has taken the same steps as others (e.g., Finland and Spain) to be ready for responses to other large-scale, large-casualty attacks.
- Spain appears, on the surface, to have been more active than any of the other countries in urging the EU to take steps in many facets of counter-terrorism. This could be an attempt by Spain to gain greater EU support for its own lengthy struggle with internal terrorism.

Section 2: Country chapters

In the following section we will provide country chapters for the countries that were studied. They are listed in alphabetical order, except Belgium, which is listed last because we were unable in the context of this quick scan to generate comparable data in relation to the other countries. The format of reporting about the selected countries (except for Belgium) follows four steps:

- General overview
  - Background
  - Reactions to 9/11
- Some characteristics of the national institutional framework
- Selected elements of national policymaking and implementation
- Matrix of challenges, measures, actors and stage

Finland[15]

General overview

Background

Finland, unlike many other European countries, has no significant experience with domestic terrorism. During the 1990´s, some radical groups (such as violent motorcycle gangs and animal liberation movements) emerged to cause problems for Finnish law enforcement authorities and policy makers. These groups cannot, however, be labelled as terrorist organisations. Also anti-globalism movements have supporters in Finland, but at least so far these groups have not caused significant problems for the authorities. International crime is present and active in Finland, mostly in the form of Russian and Estonian mafias. But although these mafias manage drug trafficking, prostitution and small-scale arms trade, so far the impact on society has been limited and no major violent disputes between rival groups have occurred. Other incidents requiring special measures – such as aircraft hijackings, assassinations of prominent individuals, or even violent bank robberies – have also been rare in Finland.

The non-existence of terrorism in Finland is almost exceptional. Reasons for this may be its stable parliamentary democracy and a somewhat remote geographical location. Also, Finland has no colonial past and no major domestic disputes between regions or population groups. The two largest minority groups, the Swedish-speaking population and the Saami people in Lapland, have extensive minority rights and are fully integrated into the Finnish society. During the Cold War (especially in the late 1940´s) it was feared that Finnish communists were planning a coup with Soviet assistance, but eventually the communists chose to use only parliamentary means to promote their political goals. There have so far been no extreme rightist or leftist movements in Finland that are worth mentioning in this context.

International terrorist groups have shown no significant interest in Finland. This may be due to not only Finland's somewhat remote geographical location but also to its modest international role in fighting international terrorism: a militarily non-aligned country, devoted to multilateralism, is not a probable target for international terrorists. This does not mean that individuals with connections to international terrorist organizations do not find their way into the country. The Finnish Security Police (Suojelupoliisi – SUPO) announced in May 2002 that one of the operational directors of a terrorist group called Abu Nidal was found to be living in

---

[15] The sources of this study consist of published news material (newspapers and magazines), official government documents (some can be found at http://formin.finland.fi/doc/eng/policies/terror.htm) and interviews with the Permanent Secretary of Ministry of Interior and the Political Under Secretary of State of Ministry for Foreign Affairs (who also acted as a deputy director of inter-ministerial working group established after 11 September attacks). Also various minor government officials provided data per e-mail and phone.

Finland at the end of 1980´s. Abu Nidal was involved in the bombing of Pan Am flight over the Scottish village of Lockerbie in 1986. The man, obviously using Finland as a base for his terrorist activities, had a Finnish passport and was married to a Finnish woman[16].

Reactions to 9/11

The attacks of 11 September showed that terrorist organisations (especially Al-Qaeda) are spread into many countries worldwide and are extremely well organised and financed. This is true for Finland as well. Individuals with connections to terrorist organizations have managed to enter Finland as well as establish themselves in the country. The confirmation for this was found in the investigations conducted after 11September that are still ongoing[17]. Latest findings of these investigations was published by SUPO in May 2002. According to this information, there are currently a few dozens individuals living in Finland that have or have had connections to international terrorist organizations. SUPO thinks that Finland does have appropriate targets, potential perpetrators and possible motives for terrorism. As SUPO sees it, some of individuals with links to terrorist organizations might be capable of perpetrating terrorist acts themselves, some not[18]. Despite this shocking information, SUPO still thinks that terrorist are not likely to attack Finnish targets and that Finland does not face any direct terrorist threat. SUPO suspects that the potential targets for terrorists in Finland are foreign embassies and international businesses with connections to the USA[19].

SUPO, however, emphasizes that there are no terrorist organizations operating in Finland. Evidently Finland is currently used as a place to establish a supportive network for terrorists. As late as in October 2001, SUPO suspected that terrorist organizations (including Al-Qaeda) use Finland as a transit country and as a place for their members to unwind. The director of SUPO stated that the reason for this could be that terrorist organisations might think that surveillance in Finland is not as strict as in other countries[20]. In the light of the latest information, it seems that Finland has a greater importance for terrorists than a mere relaxation.

Despite discovering the tracks of terrorists on Finnish soil, the Finnish authorities do not believe the country is significantly threatened by terrorism in any way. The attacks of 11 September and the discovery of individuals with connections to terrorist organisations did not radically change this belief. Some sections of administration, especially SUPO, have been closely following the activities of foreign terrorist groups for many years through relations with

---

[16] *STT* (Finnish News Agency), 20.5.2002

[17] The investigations showed also that a terrorist involved in the attacks of 11 September had applied for a visa to Finland in 2000 through the Finnish embassy in Riad, Saudi Arabia. The application was eventually turned down but the reason for this is unclear. SUPO claims that they could not be certain of the applicant's identity.

[18] *Helsingin Sanomat*, 21.5.2002

[19] *STT*, 20.5.2002, *Ilta-Sanomat* 21.5.2002

[20] *Suomen Kuvalehti*, 42/2001, pp. 14-15.

foreign intelligence services. One of the main objectives in SUPO´s fight against terrorism has been to prevent the entry of suspected terrorists to Finland, and also to keep an eye on the individuals living in Finland who have links to terrorist organisations.

The events of 11 September did, however, initiate some additional preparedness planning in Finland against terrorist attacks, since the international response forced the Finnish authorities to take terrorism seriously as well. Finland, like every other country, has emergency plans and emergency legislation in case of a crisis situation, but they are meant to be used primarily in war-like situations, such as a foreign military aggression. Preparation for terrorist attacks with weapons of mass destruction – for a strike with biological weapons, for instance – was given no special attention in the administration before 11 September. But the attacks compelled the authorities to consider such a possibility in earnest. 11 September can therefore be seen as an important impulse for the authorities to review the existing emergency plans. While many sectors of administration have been active on the matter, no completely new comprehensive plans for terrorist attacks have so far been introduced. For instance, a review conducted at the Ministry of Interior within its own jurisdiction found the existing emergency guidelines to be sufficient and led to no significant changes in them[21]. However, new measures have been undertaken to prepare for bioterrorism and information security related crime.

Although the Finnish authorities do not consider Finland as a potential target for terrorists, special working groups have been established and preventive and precautionary measures have been undertaken in various fields of administration after the events of 11 September. These will be discussed in detail in part three of this chapter. Attention will be paid also to legislation and budgetary issues as well as Finland's international contribution.

Some characteristics of the national institutional framework

The following organigram presents the relevant national actors that are dealing with counter-terrorism. On the top are bodies dealing with legislative and international aspects of terrorism. The centre level includes the executive branch. The performing actors, such as the Police Forces and SUPO, are placed at the bottom. It must be stressed that the organigram is not comprehensive. Viewed from a wide perspective, anti- and counter-terrorism activity stretches to several fields of administration at many levels. This is true for each modern state. The attached organigram merely tries to provide the reader with an overall picture of the most essential institutions.

[21] Interview with the Permanent Secretary of the Ministry of Interior.

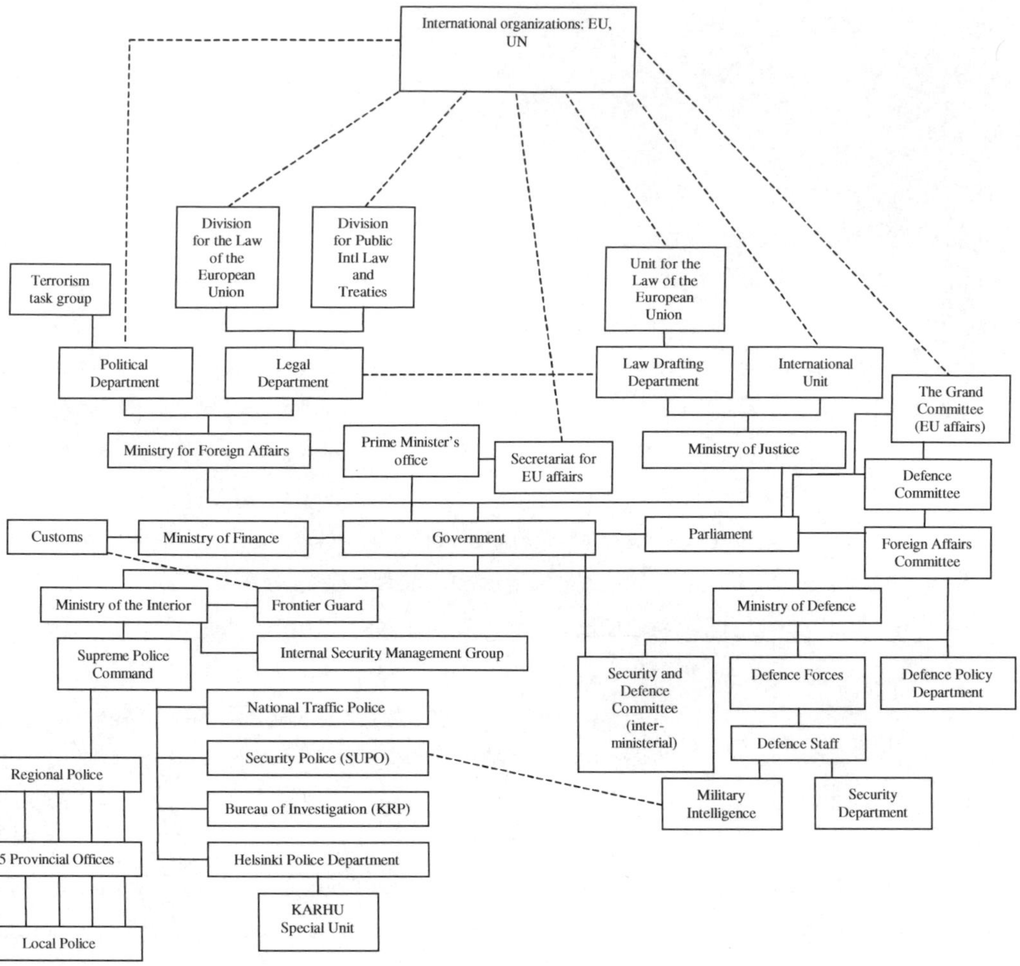

Figure 2. Organigram of relevant national actors for counter-terrorism in Finland

The Finnish administrative system is vertically oriented. Although this dates back to when Finland was under Russia's reign, the verticality is still visible. The horizontal cooperation between different branches is increasing steadily but in normal day-to-day conduct their interaction is still quite limited. Inter-ministerial working groups have been established in the fields where no single actor plays a dominant role and cross-linking cooperation is necessary. The co-operation has, however, sometimes proved to be quite difficult because competing and 'cliquish' attitudes between governmental bodies still exist. The most visible indication of the increased cooperation are the meetings of the executive-level civil servants from various ministries, who for some time now have frequently assembled in informal gatherings to discuss issues relevant to all ministries. The inter-ministerial working group that was established in the aftermath of 11 September was of this type and partly only a formalization of the existing inter-ministerial gathering. The big difference was that, this time, the group was given proper authority to implement decisions and conduct coordination. Previously the meetings had been more of a round-table discussion group where issues were only informally discussed.

In the field of counter-terrorism the ministries of Interior and Defence play a dominant role since they have responsibility for internal and national security. Because the fight against terrorism requires strong international cooperation, international organizations such as EU and UN play an increasingly important role in it. The Ministry for Foreign Affairs interacts with international bodies and shares the legislative duties with Ministry of Justice. The legislation initiated by EU and UN is filtered into Finnish legislative system through the Government and Parliament.

Ministry of Interior

The Ministry of the Interior is responsible for local and regional administration, regional development, and internal security in Finland. The Minister of the Interior also acts as the highest authority in police matters.

The Internal Security Management Group discusses strategies for public order and security and performance plans. It also coordinates security matters that belong simultaneously to several departments´ jurisdictions.

The Frontier Guard is a militarily organized troops subordinate to the Ministry of Interior. It guards the Finnish borders and carries out border checks related to controlling entry into and departure from the country at border crossing points on land borders and at sea ports and airports. The Frontier Guard is also in charge of maritime rescue service.

Finland does not have separate Special Forces solely for combating terrorism. A unit close to this definition is KARHU (bear), which is part of the police forces and designed to be used in problematic and dangerous situations such as hostage crises. It is worth mentioning that according to the existing principle, every police district is responsible for its own area. The person in charge on the crisis scene is always the local police commander if no special orders are issued. For instance, if a hostage situation breaks out in Northern Finland the regional police handles the situation unless the Supreme Police Command decides to alter the command structure (for example, send a KARHU unit to take over the situation).

Grass-root intelligence work is conducted by SUPO, which has wide international network with secret services in other countries. SUPO´s interaction with its foreign counterparts has increased enormously after 11 September. This will be discussed in a separate section later

Ministry of Defence

The Ministry of Defence is responsible for national defence policy and security and international defence policy cooperation. The Ministry is also responsible for national military defence resources and for the operating framework of the Defence Forces. The Ministry of Defence also acts as the link between the Government and the Defence Forces. The annual budget of the Ministry of Defence is about 1.7 billion Euro. Currently the national military defence expenses account for some 1.4% of GDP, which is less than in the other surveyed EU countries. The Ministry of Defence is not directly responsible for combating terrorism but it cooperates with the Ministry of Interior on matters concerning internal security. In a crisis situation, the Ministry of Defence can provide military assistance to the Police Forces. This option applies especially in situations where heavy weaponry and extra manpower are required.

Consisting of functionaries from various fields of administration, the Security and Defence Committee is an institution providing aid to the Ministry of Defence and the Cabinet Committee on Foreign and Security Policy in matters related to total national defence. The tasks of the committee are (i) to observe the changes in the position of Finland's security and defence policy and assess their effects on the arrangements of total national defence, (ii) to observe the activity in the different sectors of administration for the maintenance and development of the arrangements in total national defence, and (iii) to coordinate the preparation of matters belonging to the field of total national defence in the different sectors of administration. The committee issues statements and takes initiatives but has no executive powers.

The role of the Military Intelligence department is slightly unclear since no official information is available. The department gathers information about foreign armed forces and their activities, strength, etc., partly through forty military attachés posted abroad. Filtered information is forwarded to top decision-makers and most likely to SUPO as well.

Ministry for Foreign Affairs

An ad-hoc group for terrorism has been established under the political department of the ministry. This group, with its personnel of two, communicates the Finnish position on terrorism matters to international organisations. It has lately also taken over the work of the inter-ministerial working group as the coordinator of possible further national preventive measures.

Selected elements of national policymaking and implementation

Placed in the timeframe of six months following the attacks, the priorities of the Finnish authorities in the field of counter-terrorism were the following:[22]

[22] Provided by the Political Under Secretary of State of Ministry for Foreign Affairs.

- Repelling the threat of an attack in Finland (1-3 days after 9/11)
- Undertaking specific preventive measures to increase preparedness for, and mitigate the damage of, possible attacks (4-30 days after 9/11)
- Strengthening the international cooperation to combat world-wide terrorism (1-6 months after 9/11)

Immediate reactions on the national arena after 11 September

In the evening of 11 September the Finnish government set up a special inter-ministerial working group to co-ordinate the immediate emergency measures. The Minister of Interior Ville Itälä headed the group. It consisted of six ministers from the fields of administration most affected by the attacks (internal affairs, health and social services, foreign affairs, transport and communication, regional and municipal affairs and defence). Another working group of executive-level government functionaries from various ministries was also established to support the work of the minister group and implement the decisions. This group was named after its chairman Rauno Saari, the Secretary of State at Prime Minister's office.

Police and defence forces were put in a state of higher preparedness and the air force tightened up its control of Finnish airspace. Some special objects (US, British and Israeli embassies, places of worship, nuclear power plants) were placed under special protection. Border control as well as security checks at the airports were immediately tightened. SUPO was ordered to prepare a threat-analysis of potential terrorist targets in Finland, identifying possible special precautions needed to cope with the situation. The National Bureau of Investigation (Keskusrikospoliisi – KRP) and SUPO intensified connections and correspondence with their foreign counterparts and international police organizations to ensure faster exchange of information. On September 12, SUPO stated that Finland is not under direct terrorist threat because, according to minister Itälä, who was informing the press on SUPO´s findings, the attacks a day earlier were directed solely against the US government and American institutions[23] .

Measures undertaken within a few months after 11 September

The minister group headed by Itälä was soon abolished and the longer-term coordination was transferred to Saari´s working group. The group consisted of twenty-two top civil servants from various ministries. The mission of this group was to co-ordinate and supervise the counter-terrorism activity of different governmental bodies and to survey the Finnish legislation for necessary additions concerning terrorist threat and prepare response measures against possible attacks. The group brought the ministries together and served also as a means to deliver information from one ministry to another. The government, politicians, and the public were also informed about the activities of Saari´s group.

[23] *Helsingin Sanomat,* 13.9.2001.

Saari´s group initiated precautionary measures in different sectors of administration within four weeks of the attacks. The group itself did not make these decisions, but instead acted primarily as a co-ordinating force. Each ministry was responsible for taking the necessary action in its own administrative sector. As of now, Saari´s group has not been officially abolished but its work has been transferred to the ad-hoc group (mentioned earlier) that works under the Ministry for Foreign Affairs.

The following measures were undertaken within four weeks after the attacks of 11 September:

- Security measures in the field of aviation were strengthened. This is the field most affected by the attacks of 11 September. Finnair, the national air carrier, announced that it would replace the cockpit doors with bulletproof ones. Security checks are now conducted also on domestic flights. A review of the national emergency plan for cases of hijacked aircraft was initiated in cooperation between the police, the Defence forces, the Frontier Guard, and Finnair.
- Finnair is introducing a biometric fingerprint identification system to validate the identity of flight crew members. Negotiations about the practical arrangements with Frontier Guard are underway and the system should be in use by the end of 2003. The procedure will eventually be extended to passengers but there are yet no estimates when this will take place. Finnair started the development of the identification system already in the spring of 2001 but the events of 11 September have speeded up the development process.
- Tightened border control was maintained throughout the fall along the borders and at airports as well as sea harbours. This was due not only to the events of 11 September but also to the US operation in Afghanistan. The increased control was quite easy to implement because the volume of incoming traffic to Finland is low. The road traffic comes mainly from Russia through Finland's' eastern border; in practice, incoming cars were screened more thoroughly and individuals of some nationalities were subjected to tighter checks than before.
- The Finnish Customs continued to carry out a stricter control of transported goods and the Directorate of Immigration started paying more attention to the methods of processing of applications.
- In the field of rescue services, collaboration between the competent authorities was intensified and local emergency plans were reviewed.
- The health care authorities increased their preparedness for attacks utilizing biological weapons. Hospitals were advised to ensure an appropriate supply of medicines. No action was taken to prepare for chemical or nuclear attacks, but

additional security precautions were introduced in Finland's four nuclear power plants. For instance, no 'unknown' visitors are admitted to the plants[24].

- The Defence Forces started to develop 'quick test' measures for identification of biological weapons.
- A special advisory board on information security was set up. Information security experts at the Finnish Communications Regulatory Authority (Viestintävirasto) were ordered to be on alert 24 hours a day as of January 1, 2002. More attention was also given to the work of the Computer Emergency Response Team (CERT).
- The defence administration increased the level of protection within its own entities and was prepared to permanently intensify cooperation with other national authorities in eliminating the threat of terrorism.
- The Ministry of Defence and the Defence Forces were prepared to apply a rapid procedure to issue authorizations for flights through the Finnish airspace. This refers to the possible need for the US aircraft to fly over the Finnish airspace en route to Afghanistan. However, Finland was willing to grant permits only for humanitarian flights over its country.
- The Financial Supervision Authority (Rahoitustarkastuskeskus – RATA) investigated, in cooperation with Finnish banks, the possible financial links of terrorist groups to Finland. The investigations showed no signs of such connections.
- The Finnish Post issued new safety instructions for handling suspicious mail after letters containing white powder were discovered also in Finland[25]. Postal workers would have been given antibiotics in case of an anthrax infection. Domestic airfreight will be subjected to tighter checks than before.

SUPO´s activities

SUPO continued to investigate the links of the international terrorist organisations to Finland and further intensified its foreign connections after 11 September. As a result to the attacks, SUPO suddenly faced a considerably bigger amount of work tasks and it is easy to assume that SUPO was not quite prepared to this. Limited resources and massively increased workload caused jams on some sectors of activity and eventually resulted to pile-ups. The situation was worsened by the transfer of SUPO´s two head analysts to EUROPOL[26]. The Following matrix demonstrates the state of SUPO´s work assignments at the end of October 2002:

---

[24] Nuclear safety has been on the agenda lately because Finland is currently planning to build a fifth nuclear reactor. The parliament will vote on the issue at the end of May 2002.

[25] The white powder found in the letters tested negative for anthrax.

[26] *Ilta-Sanomat*, 21.5.2002

Task	State of assignment		
	Under control	Jammed	Critical
Use of public sources	X		
International meetings and conferences			X
Gathering, analysing and reporting information			X
Receiving and verifying possible clues			X
'Human interest' (usage of informers)			X
Tailing tasks		X	
Technical data acquisition	X		
Acquisition of other information (authorities, civilians, communities)		X	
Supportive assignments			X
Public relations	X		
International co-operation			X
Security surveillance	X		
Investigation	X		

Figure 3. State of SUPO´s assignments at the end of October 2002[27].

Legislation

Prior to 11 September, Finland had signed all twelve UN conventions on terrorism and ratified nine of them. One additional convention[28] was ratified in December 2001 and the last two conventions[29] will be ratified during 2002. One chapter of the penal code must be amended before the convention on financing of terrorism can enter into force. This will take place in the autumn of 2002.

Finland itself does not have any specific counter terrorist legislation. According to the existing legislation, terrorism is classified as a police matter. After 11 September, the Finnish authorities found no immediate need to alter or amend the legislation. Officials of the US embassy tried to persuade the authorities to initiate a special counter terrorist legislation but Finland decided to wait for the reactions of the EU, which soon actualised. A separate chapter on terrorist offences will be added to the penal code during 2002 in context of the national implementation of the EU Framework Decision on Terrorism. The Ministry of Defence did, however, review applicable national statutes, which may have needed amendments in order to make combating terrorism more effective[30]. Even though the government acknowledges the need to define more specifically the powers of the Defence Forces in situations where terrorist attacks are directed against Finland or where there is a threat of such attacks, the

[27] Matrix was originally published first in *Helsingin Sanomat*, 21.5.2002

[28] The Convention on the Marking of Plastic Explosives for the Purpose of Detection.

[29] The International Convention for the Suppression of the Financing of Terrorism and the International Convention for the Suppression of Terrorist Bombings.

[30] These statutes include the Territorial Surveillance Act, the Act on the Export and Transit of Defence Materiel, and the Act on the Provision of Assistance by the Defence Forces for the Police.

government decided that there is no immediate need to alter the existing legislation on these matters for the moment.

The EU Framework Decision on Terrorism raises some minor issues about the existing Finnish legislation, mainly with respect to the maximum legal punishment and deportation of Finnish citizens to another, non-EU country. In the EU framework, the maximum punishment for terrorist crimes is 15 years, whereas the current Finnish legislation allows no punishments longer than 12 years. This problem will be solved by a simple mathematical trick: because a person charged with terrorist crimes is likely to have committed other serious crimes as well, the person can be sentenced for an extra three years to prison. This would total the 15 years required by the EU Framework. Deportation of Finnish citizens to a third country outside the EU (more specifically the US) will only be possible if guarantees are given that the death penalty will not be sought. The EU Framework will be implemented and the necessary modifications to the national legislation made during 2002.

One temporary problem caused by the EU Framework Decision on Terrorism is that the ongoing preparations for the implementation of the framework have badly blocked the national law drafting system. The EU framework is considered to be more urgent than other national law drafting and therefore many national laws waiting to be processed through the drafting system have been put on hold.

Budgetary information

Since no major changes have been made by the administration, the costs of the activities undertaken in the aftermath of 11 September are not very significant. The basic rule that applies to most fields of administration is that, whatever measures were taken, they were taken within the existing budget frames. Many ministries and other governmental bodies did find it difficult to handle increased work duties without extra funds, and in many branches of administration the internal cash flow system was slightly altered. Tasks that were less urgent were suddenly left without money because the funds were redirected to counter terrorist measures. Exceptions can, however, be found in some fields.

Tightened security checks at the Finnish airports have required investments in new equipment; new staff has also been recruited. The cost of the investments at the airports has so far been 24,2 million Euro. Expenditures for extra staff will be around 10 million Euro per year.

The raised security level has so far cost Finnair approximately 4,7 million Euro. Additional insurance payments total a further 3,4 million Euro. Investments needed to enhance security of the entire Finnair fleet are yet to come; the current minimum estimate is 2 million Euro.

Investments for enhancing the security arrangements on passenger ships are planned. No information about the costs is available.

Additional investments have been made on the field of information security, but unfortunately no data on these investments are available yet. Investments have also been made in companies that are providing information security solutions (F-Secure, Nokia, Sonera) but no information about the sums invested have been made public at this moment.

Frontier Guard and SUPO were issued extra funds to cover the costs of increased activity[31].

Police Forces will get some compensation (200.000-300.000 Euro) for guarding three foreign embassies around the clock. No new personnel has been recruited to Police Forces.

The National Public Health Institute invested 20.000 Euro for Biological warfare preparation research. In addition, 840.000 Euro will be requested within next year's budget frames for further preventive measures.

The Finnish Post estimates that the delivery cut-offs caused by hoax powder letters cost the company around 170.000 Euro. Negotiations are underway between the Finnish Post and Civil Aviation Authority about the investments needed to screen domestic airfreight. There is yet no information available about the funds needed for the investments.

Participation in the ISAF peacekeeping mission in Afghanistan costs Finland approximately 3,6 million Euro.

International activity

In spite of being fortunate in lacking operational terrorist activity so far, Finland has been active in the international arena in condemning terrorism in all its forms. The Finnish position is that terrorism is a threat to the implementation of human rights, democracy and the rule of law as well as to international peace and security. In the fight against terrorism, Finland underlines the importance of international cooperation, collective action, respect for human rights, and the rule of law. Finland stresses the importance of the UN in actions against terrorism and calls for strengthening the role of UN conventions. Finland itself has already ratified ten of a total of twelve UN conventions against terrorism, as stated above.

As a member of the European Union, Finland has closely cooperated in the suppression of terrorism within the framework of Common Foreign and Security Policy and Home and Justice

---

[31] No specific sums are available but a high government official called the extra funds issued as "peanuts".

affairs. The Action plan adopted at the Laeken European Council in mid-December is currently being processed in the law drafting bodies.

After the attacks of 11 September, the Finnish role in the international fight against terrorism has, however, been quite limited. Finland naturally quickly condemned the attacks and united with the world in the fight against terrorism. On the operational level the Finnish contribution has been mostly supportive. Since Finland is not a NATO member, the activation of the fifth article of NATO charter affected it little. Finland did not, consequently, take part in the military operation against the Taliban in Afghanistan[32]. In the context of preparations for a long-term action plan to combat terrorism that NATO has initiated, Finland has made its contribution through the Euro-Atlantic Partnership Council (EAPC), of which it is a member.

Conclusions

With regard to the framework of this study, Finland has deployed limited counter-terrorism policies since the events of 11 September as well as prior to that. This may partly be due to the belief of the Finnish authorities that Finland is not a likely target for either domestic or international terrorists. Key officials interviewed by us hesitate to speculate about domestic trans-attack and post-attack responses. The common belief that terrorism does not pose a threat to Finland has resulted in the fact that no significant changes in the existing emergency plans and no completely new emergency plans have been made in the administration after the attacks of 11 September. The existing emergency planning, which mainly focuses on preparation for a foreign military strike, was considered sufficient to cover also possible major terrorist attacks. If we look at the relative importance that this position places on emergency planning for pre-, trans- and post-attack phases, we can conclude that Finland concentrates its efforts almost solely on the pre-attack phase. Some limited preparedness planning, especially in the field of information security, aviation, and health services has been initiated. Also SUPO has intensified its activities within Finland and intensified active cooperation with its sister organizations abroad. All of these can be categorised as pre-attack, tactical and operational activities that are not specific to any particular challenge.

The current risk assessment by the authorities considers foreign institutions located in Finland as the only possible targets for terrorists. This assessment reflects the tension in the Middle East and the situation in Afghanistan. Representatives of the warring parties as well as companies originating from the countries involved in these two conflicts are seen as the most potential targets. Measures are undertaken accordingly to prevent possible attacks.

When asked about responses to future terrorism scenarios involving Finnish targets, the authorities often choose to decline comment. Some consider the decision-making system,

[32] Finland is participating in the international peacekeeping mission in Afghanistan as part of the ISAF troops.

technical infrastructures, and other non-human assets as the more likely terrorist targets than prominent individuals or large human masses. Ministers and other important politicians do not even have bodyguards (except the Prime Minister and the President) because, firstly, there is no evidence that their safety is in jeopardy and, secondly, providing bodyguards would require considerable funds. One indication of the authorities´ attitude towards terrorism is that different sorts of 'lunatics' are considered more of a threat than hardcore terrorists. For instance, media hype can influence unstable persons to commit irrational acts such as sending copycat hoax powder letters. The targets of these 'lunatics' are hard to predict beforehand and thus they can cause nasty and unwanted surprises.

As far as the government actors are concerned, no special arrangements have been made after 11 September other than the establishment of a ministerial committee and a two-man working group. The issue of terrorism stretches widely across the areas of many governmental bodies. A coordination initiative covering all these relevant administrative sectors has therefore been regarded as necessary. This has had little effect on the work of the different institutions, however. The 'rule of thumb' still is that actors are responsible for the tasks that are assigned to them by law.

On an everyday basis, the most important actor level in counter-terrorism action in Finland is federal. The different ministries are responsible for initiating and performing activities in their legislative fields. Various departments and other actors subordinate to ministries perform the actions initiated by the ministries. Executive branch, the government, is eventually in charge of the affairs and can initiate action if necessary. The parliament is the supreme legislative body. SUPO, however, is an exception to the rule. It has great autonomy and can go about its activities somewhat independently.

On the other hand, it is difficult to predict if and how the administration would be rearranged should a major terrorist homeland attack occur. As noted earlier, the vertical orientation of the Finnish administrative structure is likely to create obstacles for effective coordination when a broad issue affecting many fields of administration, such as the new terrorism, emerges on the agenda. In this light it is safe to assume – depending on the nature and gravity of the attack, of course – that also in a Finnish crisis situation a working group bringing all various sections of administration together would be established. This would ensure smooth operability and prevent overlap and confusion.

Although Finland has taken no radical steps to prepare for terrorist strikes, and although in general business goes on as usual, the attacks of 11 September and their effects on Finland have taught two important lessons to the administration. Firstly, and most importantly, the cooperation between the ministries and departments increased significantly. Saari´s group succeeded in its mission to bring the highest-ranking officials from various ministries to the table to effectively work together as a team. Government functionaries welcomed the new teamwork mentality, and many wish to continue and even improve this new administrative trend. This is clearly a phenomenon that will have long-term effects on the Finnish administrative system.

Secondly, the authorities started to take preventive action against possible attacks where biological weapons are used. Although the threat is extremely small, the public health administration participated in the activities of Saari´s group from the very beginning. Therefore we can conclude that Finland did relatively well in this field.

Despite these two improvements, one high government official expressed concern about the terrorists´ relative freedom to operate in Finland. According to this official, operating in Finland would be easy, mainly because the Finnish authorities do not consider the large-scale penetration of terrorist organisations to Finland as a real possibility. Luckily there has so far been no indication of this. Regardless, one should bear in mind that there are individuals with connections to terrorist organizations present and living in the country. Behaviour of these individuals is hard to predict.

Matrix of Finland's challenges, measures, actors, stages and progress

CHS: Challenges as outlined
Msrs: Measures 1-Strategic, 2-Operational, 3-Tactical
Actors: 1-Public sector, federal/national level, civil (including special forces), 2-Public sector, 3-Regional/state level, civil, 4-Public sector, local level, civil, 5-Military, 6-Private sector
Sgs: Stages: 1-pre-attack, 2-trans-attack, 3-post-attack
Pgs: Progress: 1-No specific post 9/11 action; 2-Need for action identified, policy in the making; 3-Budget appropriated, actors identified; 4-Policy implementation well underway; 5-Policy implementation finalised

Nr	Description Finland post 9/11 policymaking and –implementation	Chs	Mrs	Ars	Sgs	Remarks (budgets in rounded figures)	Pgs
AVIATION AND MARITIME SECURITY							
1	Higher security level in the field of aviation		2	1, 5	1-3	(4,7 million Euro for Finnair, additional insurance payments 3,4 million Euro)	5
2	Investments to equipment for stricter screening of baggage and passengers		3	1, 5	1	(24,2 million Euro total)	4
3	Security checks also on domestic flights; recruitment of additional security staff		3	1, 5	1	(10 million Euro/year)	4
4	Airfreight screened on domestic flights		3	1, 5	1	Negotiations about the financing of new equipment underway between the Finnish Post and the Civil Aviation Authority	2
5	Investments to Finnair fleet for enhanced security		3	1, 5	1-3	The only measure published so far is that the cockpit doors will be replaced by bulletproof ones (minimum estimate 2 million Euro)	2
6	Review of emergency plan for cases of aircraft hijackings		2	1, 5	1	(N/A)	5
7	Investments for enhancing security arrangements on passenger ships		3	1, 5	1-3	planned, (N/A)	2
DEFENCE							
8	Development of quick test measures for identification of biological weapons	2, 4	3	4	1-2	(N/A)	4
9	Preparations to apply a rapid procedure to issue authorizations for flights en route to Afghanistan		3	1, 4	2	Finland allows only humanitarian overflights	5
10	Increased protection of entities and depots of the Defence Forces		3	4	1	(N/A)	5
11	Preparedness to intensify cooperation with other national authorities in combating terrorism		2	1, 4	1-3	(N/A)	5
INTERIOR							
12	24 hour police surveillance of three foreign embassies in Finland		3	3	1	US, Britain, Israel (200 000-300 000 Euro)	5
13	Increased security level at Finnish embassies abroad		3	1	1	(N/A)	5
14	Tightened border control along the outer borders, at airports and at harbours		3	1, 3	1	(N/A)	5
15	Stricter control of transported goods		3	1, 3	1	(N/A)	5
16	Attention to the methods of processing visa applications		2	1	1	(N/A)	5
17	Review of emergency plans in field of rescue services and increase of collaboration between competent authorities		2	1, 3	1-3	(N/A)	5
18	Constant update of terrorism threat analysis by SUPO		1	1	1	(N/A)	4
19	Intensified cooperation between SUPO and its foreign counterparts		2	1	1	(N/A)	5
20	More resources for SUPO to cover intensified activity		2	1	1-2	(small sums)l	4
21	Intensified cooperation between KRP and international police organizations		2	1	1	(N/A)	5
22	Tightened security measures at nuclear power	2, 4	3	1	1-3	(N/A)	5

	plants						
LEGISLATIVE ISSUES							
23	Ratification of the UN conventions on terrorism		2	1	1	One convention ratified in December 2001, the final two will be ratified during 2002	4
24	Rapid ratification of the EU Framework Decision on Terrorism and necessary modifications to national legislation		2	1	1-3	During 2002	4
25	Review of existing legislation for necessary amendments on terrorism		2	1	1	(N/A)	5
26	Review of the statutes on cooperation between Defence Forces and authorities responsible of internal security		2	1, 4	1-3	(N/A)	5
HEALTH							
27	Increased preparedness for in case of an attack utilizing biological weapons	2, 4	1	1	1-2	(N/A)	3
28	Hospital advised to ensure an appropriate supply of medicines	2, 4	3	1, 3	1-2	(N/A)	5
29	Research project on biological warfare preparations	2, 4	2	1	1	(20 000 Euro, 840 000 Euro requested for next year)	3
30	New safety instructions for postal workers for handling suspicious mail	2	3	5	1	In particular for handling letters containing powder	5
FINANCE							
31	Investigation of possible financial links of terrorist organizations to Finland		3	1	1	(N/A)	5
INFORMATION SECURITY							
32	Setting up a special advisory board on information security	2, 4, 6	1	1	1-3	(N/A)	5
33	More attention to work of the CERT team	2, 4, 6	2	1	1-3	(N/A)	4
34	Information security expert on call 24 hours a day as of 1.1.2002	2, 4, 6	3	1	1	(N/A)	5
FOREIGN AFFAIRS							
35	Foster international cooperation to combat terrorism		1	1	1	(N/A)	2
36	Active participation to a/c terrorism activities of the UN, EU and EAPC		1	1	1	(N/A)	2
37	Participation to ISAF peace-keeping operation in Afghanistan		3	1	3	(N/A)	5
ADMINISTRATION							
38	Establishment of a high-level inter-ministerial working group for coordinating the measures of various governmental bodies on a/c terrorism		2	1	1-3	(N/A)	5
39	Permanent intensified cooperation between ministries on matters concerning a/c terrorism		1, 2	1	1-3	(N/A)	2
40	Establishment of an ad-hoc working group for communicating Finnish views on terrorism to international organizations		2	1	1-3	(N/A)	5

France

General overview

Background

Like several other European countries, France has been a victim of international terrorism on its homeland territory and abroad for many years. Among others, it faces threats from Islamic militant cells belonging to the Armed Islamic Group (GIA) and Salafist Preaching and Combat Group (SPCG). Other notable terrorist networks operating in France include ETA and the National Liberation Front of Corsica (FLNC). To better protect itself against terrorist threats, France has equipped itself with an important anti-terrorist arsenal based on two main pillars: one of operational prevention and repression ('Vigipirate'), and a legislative pillar (based on the September 9th Act of 1986).

'Vigipirate' was conceived in 1978 during the first wave of terrorist attacks in Europe (Rote Armee Fraktion in Germany and the Red Brigades in Italy) as the French government's main plan for preventing threats and reacting against actions by terrorists. The document itself is classified, but its goal is to mobilise all the police and military to strengthen security. It allows deployment of personnel from branches of the French Armed Forces (soldiers, gendarmes, and paratroopers) to assist specially assigned local law enforcement personnel from national and municipal police forces. They patrol and check critical and sensitive areas; most notably those frequented by the public in Paris and elsewhere in France (airports, train stations, public transportation and other public areas). There are two stages: 'Vigipirate simple' and 'Vigipirate renforcé', in which the armed forces participate. Vigipirate was activated for the first time in 1991 during the Gulf War (the reinforced stage for four months), and was never deactivated since, only stepped down to 'simple' and then stepped up again in 1995 and 1996 after some terrorist attacks, during the 1998 World Cup to counter threats from Algerian extremists, during the Kosovo crisis and in November 2000 in Corsica[33]. Besides Vigipirate, France also has a number of emergency plans in case of a chemical (Piratox) or nuclear (Piratome) accident or attack, and for both airplane (Piratair) and ship (Pirate-mer) hijackings[34].

France is one of six EU countries that have a specific anti-terrorist legislation, the cornerstone of which is the September 9th Act of 1986, providing for the prosecution of all terrorist acts. Under this Act, terrorism is defined as an infraction committed by an individual, or a group of individuals, aimed at seriously disrupting public order through intimidation or terror. Terrorist

[33] For more information on Vigipirate, see
http://www.servicepublic.fr/accueil/vigipirate_definition.html and
http://www.defence.gouv.fr/actualites/publications/defactu/n74/dossier.html
[34] http://www.consulfrance-quebec.org/Presse/Dossiers/wtc/france.htm.

crimes are subject to a special and harsher legal procedure, and also carry some of the longest penalties in the French legal system (up to 30 years imprisonment)[35].

Reactions to 9/11

France adopted several plans and measures after 11 Septemberth—principally, they aim to strengthen homeland defence and increase vigilance.

The Vigipirate Renforcé Plan (VRP)—Ensuring Physical Protection

Former Prime Minister Jospin activated the Vigipirate Renforcé Plan on September 12th as a response to the terrorist attacks in the United States. The Minister of Interior instructed the prefects to strengthen surveillance and controls around American and Israeli diplomatic premises and in airports, stations, public transport and public buildings that could be potential targets[36]. Then Defence Minister Alain Richard instituted a reinforced air defence consisting of four patrols of fighter jets on ready alert to intercept intrusions of French air space. The Defence Ministry also boosted security at sensitive locations such as nuclear plants, large dams and major industrial installations.

The Prefect of Paris Police, Jean-Paul Prost, announced increased security measures around diplomatic postings with particular emphasis on the US and Israeli embassies.[37] French prefectures received the order to implement Phase II (highest alert) of the Plan within 48 hours. On September 13th, Interior Minister Daniel Vaillant assembled the Counter-terrorism Ministerial Committee (CILAT) and unveiled the main elements of Vigipirate. On 7 October, these measures were reinforced[38].

Phase II of Vigipirate calls for enhanced awareness among all public services and private partners to increase security along French highways, train stations, metro, ports, airports, schools, and shopping centres. Other secured areas include tourist sites, museums, theatres and places of worship. The current measures will be in place for two years, until December 31st 2003.

---

[35] In particular: the centralization of instruction and sentencing in a special centralized court in Paris, the extension to four days of the maximum duration of police custody, the possibility of carrying out searches at night, postponement of the intervention of a lawyer until after 72 hour of police custody, trial of terrorist crimes by a special court made up of professional magistrates and finally of a device in favour of 'repentants' (special sentence reductions for repentant terrorists that allow for the prevention of terrorist acts, leading to the avoidance of loss of human life).

[36] Intervention de Monsieur le Ministre de l'Intérieur devant la commission de la défense nationale et de la commission des affaires étrangères (Assemblée nationale), 14 septembre 2001. For an English version, see http://www.assemblee-nat.fr/dossiers/attentats/attentats-2.asp

[37] We are grateful to RAND visiting fellow Bénédicte Suzan for information on the measures implemented by Defence Minister Richard and Mr. Jean-Paul Prost. The section on the Biotox Plan also leans on information provided in her unpublished paper entitled "French Perspectives on Counter-terrorism and the International Coalition", prepared for RAND in April 2002.

[38] For an overview of these additional measures, see the website of the French Prime Minister: http://www.premier-ministre.gouv.fr/fr/p.cfm?ref=28340&txt=1.

Under VRP, some 5400 additional police, gendarmes or other military personnel have been assigned to anti-terrorist patrols and domestic security throughout France. In Paris, about 600 soldiers, 850 paratroopers and 1,300 gendarmes have reinforced the plan, thus bringing the total to some 7,000 mobilized military and security forces. Moreover, France has almost 5,000 personnel engaged in the US-led campaign against Al-Qaeda and Taliban forces in Afghanistan. These are mostly crew members of the five ships in the task force led by the Charles de Gaulle aircraft carrier, plus an unspecified number of French Special Forces personnel on the ground in Afghanistan[39].

Biotox Plan—Addressing Biological Threats

Under the auspices of the Ministry of Health, the Biotox Plan on biological risk complements the VRP through specific measures in the areas of prevention, surveillance, early warning, and emergency action[40]. It stems from an inter-ministerial effort commenced in 1999 and adopted in October 2001. The Biotox Plan calls for closer cooperation between civilian and military agencies concerned with biological threats. Its budget is approximately 60 million Euro. New arrangements were incorporated on September 22nd 2001, to increase security at facilities for the production, storage and transport of hazardous biological materials. These include:

- Adding several agents of infectious diseases and pathogenic microorganisms to the list of poisonous substances.
- Modifying protocols for import, possession, transfer, acquisition, and transport of agents of certain infectious diseases, pathogenic microorganisms, and toxins[41].

FINTER—Financial Surveillance

On September 20th 2001, the Ministry of Economic Affairs, Finance, and Industry established an ad hoc coordinating group (FINTER), to strengthen harmonization between French economic and financial agencies with competencies in the area of monetary surveillance. Given UN Resolution 1373, one of the principal objectives of FINTER is to uncover and freeze terrorists' assets[42]. As of December 2001, France had frozen about 4.42 million Euro worth of funds traced to Taliban members.

Loi sur la Sécurité Quotidienne—Law on Everyday Security

On November 15th 2001, the French Parliament passed the law on everyday security. It calls for more proactive measures to curb potential terrorist activities. The general objectives are:

---

[39] Jane's Information Group 2002.

[40] Biotox forms part of the larger Piratox Plan under Vigipirate. Piratox was established in the early 1990s. http://www.sante.gouv.fr/htm/dossiers/biotox/

[41] United Nations Security Council (S/2001/1274) "Letter dated 27 December 2001 from the Chairman of the Security Council Committee established pursuant to resolution 1373 (2001) concerning counter-terrorism addressed to the President of the Security Council, p. 15.

[42] The ministries involved include Treasury, Customs, Taxes, Fiscal, External Economic Relations, and Judicial Affairs.

- More effective handling of offences that may be connected to terrorist activities;
- Intensifying use of technology in the fight against terrorism;
- Establishing a special definition of the offence of financing terrorist activity;
- Bringing insider trading and money-laundering within the list of acts of terrorism; and
- Imposing an additional penalty involving the confiscation of the assets of terrorist and a provision providing for interim protective measures against the offender's assets[43].

Some characteristics of the national institutional framework

France does not have a particular government department with the sole responsibility of combating terrorism. Rather, anti-terror efforts involve the mobilisation of all relevant departments available to contribute to its prevention and suppression.

The organigram (Figure 4) provides a simple overview of the French agencies involved in counter-terrorism[44]. It should be noted that not all groups are identified. For example, TRACFIN (Treatment of Information and Action Against Clandestine Financial Circuits) within the Ministry of Economic Affairs, Finance, and Industry and the Foreign Ministry's Department of Strategic Security and Disarmament and are not included[45]. This basic organisational structure focuses on the elements organised under the Ministry of Defence and Ministry of the Interior.

---

[43] Ibid, p. 6.

[44] Sources used in creating this figure include the Federation of American Scientists, the French Interior Ministry, and Jane's Information Group.

[45] Similarly, this section does not include a representation of the *Tribunal de Grande Instance de Paris* that houses the investigative magistrates.

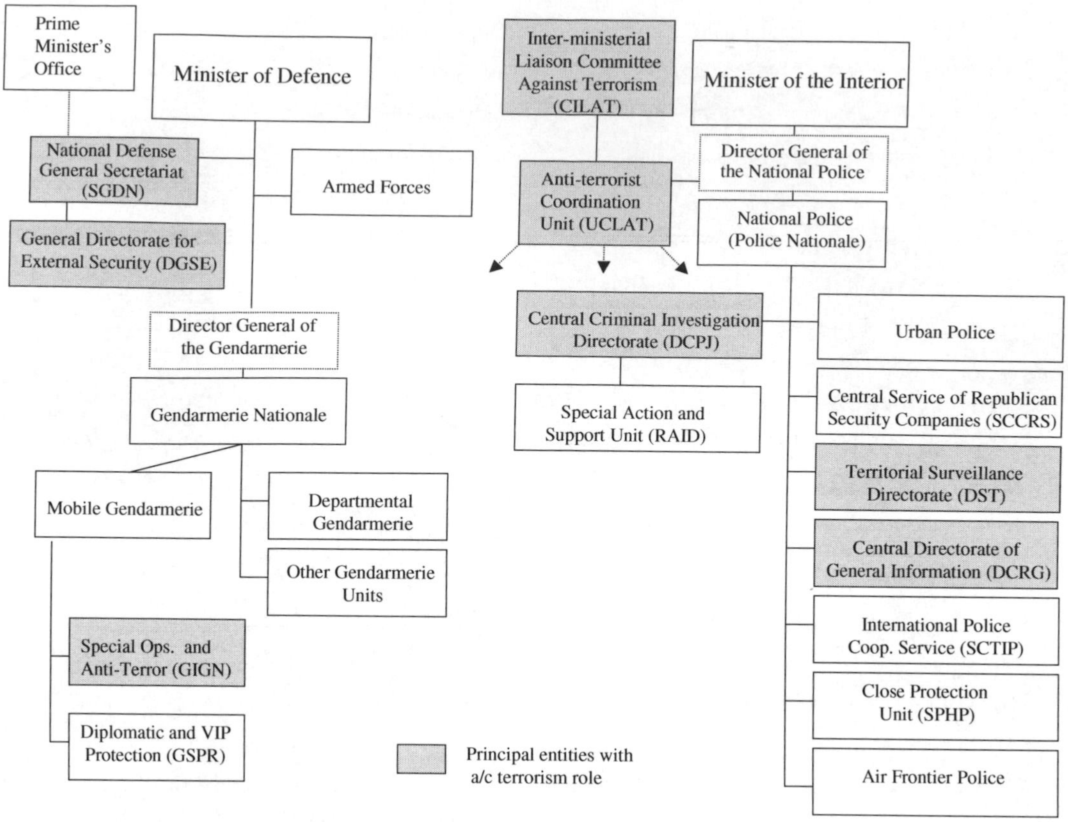

Figure 4- Organigram of Relevant French Agencies Concerned with Counter-terrorism

Ministry of Defence

The Ministry of Defence has authority over the armed forces, the Gendarmerie, and the General Directorate for External Security (DGSE). DGSE is responsible for collecting and sorting raw electronic and military intelligence. DSGE also conducts counter espionage outside France. Known as the French foreign intelligence agency, it answers only to French presidents and prime ministers.

The Gendarmerie Nationale enforces the law and guarantees public security. It polices some 95 percent of France, including all towns with less than 10,000 inhabitants. It includes three major components: the Mobile Gendarmerie (riot police who can be deployed anywhere in the country), the Departmental Gendarmerie (who operate from fixed points), and other Gendarmerie units (e.g. Gendarmerie de l'Air, Republican Guard, Gendarmerie Maritime, Gendarmerie de l'Armament). The Special Operations and Anti-terror unit (GIGN), under the Mobile Gendarmerie, is a specialized operational police unit designed to handle high-risk security threats.

The Ministry of the Interior

The Ministry of the Interior is responsible for the maintenance and cohesion of the country's institutions throughout France. The Minister of the Interior covers areas such as law and order, public safety, public freedoms, elections, and local authorities.

The director general of the National Police has authority over the Counter Terrorist Coordination Unit (UCLAT). UCLAT, among others, is responsible for ensuring cross cutting exchange of information and analysis between all actors involved in the fight against terrorism. Reporting to the Minister of the Interior, the director general also Commands the National Police. This force operates primarily in urban areas with over 100,000 inhabitants. As shown in the organigram, a host of organizations make up the National Police. The most relevant in combating terrorism are:

- The Directorate of Territorial Security (DST): With about 1,500 personnel, DST is responsible for counter terrorist activities throughout France. Previously focusing on counter-intelligence, the group now tracks foreign criminals and terrorists operating in France. As such, there is growing cooperation between the DST and DGSE.
- The Central General Intelligence Directorate or Renseignements Generaux (DCRG or RG): This political intelligence unit collects information on groups considered to be threats to national security. About 4,000 individuals work for the DCRG—700 of these are assigned to the Prefecture of Police of Paris.
- The Central Criminal Investigation Directorate (DCPJ): Also known as the Judicial Police, the DCPJ handles economic, financial, criminal, technical, and scientific crime. It conducts a significant portion of all national criminal investigations. The 6th division of the DCPJ has as its mission to detect and prevent subversive and terrorist activities. The DCPJ's director is the nation's chief detective and the head of the French section of Interpol.
- RAID (Special Action and Support Unit) is under the DCPJ and represents France's second specialized operational police unit for security. Both GIGN and RAID were fully mobilized post 9/11 under the Vigipirate Renforcé Plan.

Coordination

The Council for Interior Security (Conseil de Sécurité Intérieur, created in 1997) is chaired by the Prime Minister, and is composed of the Ministers of the Interior, Justice, Defence, Foreign Affairs and Finances. It evaluates threats that could touch the national territory, and adapts the anti-terrorist instruments. The political coordination of anti-terrorist policy rests with the Interministerial Liaison Committee Against Terrorism (Comité Interministériel de Lutte Anti-Terroriste - CILAT), a high level committee that meets on average twice a year and coordinates the activities of all relevant ministries involved in the combat against terrorism. It includes the Prime Minister and Ministers of Interior, Defence, Justice, and Foreign Affairs.

CILAT is in turn responsible for the Anti-Terrorism Coordination Unit (Unité de Coordination de la Lutte Anti-Terroriste), a working level coordination group that includes agencies from the Ministries of Interior and Defence that coordinate operations and resides organisationally within the Ministry of Interior[46].

In times of crisis, the joint operational centre (centre opérationnel interarmées - COIA) of the Ministry of Defence, in connection with the operational centre of inter-ministerial crisis management (Centre opérationnel de gestion interministérielle des crises - COGIC) of the ministry for the Interior, evaluate the situation and define the response.

Selected elements of national policymaking and implementation

Given its long-standing experience with terrorism, France has historically had a strong arsenal of anti-terrorist policies and measures. For example, even before the 11 September[th] attacks, the Ministry of Justice allowed for legal procedures authorizing the arrest of potential terrorists before they could carry out their attacks. As such, France's policymaking and implementation post 9/11 has primarily involved the activation of preconceived contingency plans to bolster security and providing agencies with anti-terrorism roles more freedom of action to prevent attacks. The descriptions below are a continuation of those described in the earlier section (Reactions to 9/11).

Air Safety and Border Control Measures

One of the first measures implemented post 9/11—besides securing certain critical infrastructure and other significant structures—concerned air travel. Consistent with policy implementations in other countries, a variety of security measures were modified and reviewed post 9/11 to ensure that a similar terrorist attack using aircraft as a weapon would not be replicated in France. The new procedures place more emphasis on careful screening of passengers and their luggage, especially hand luggage. There is greater control of personnel access at the hubs of major airports, enhanced aircraft access control, and improved methods for the inspection of freight and catering supplies[47].

In a similar vain, policies were modified to secure vulnerable entry points. For example, customs service now conducts special security inspections of all passenger, tourist vehicle, trucking and railway freight traffic going through the Channel Tunnel to The UK. While these inspections were already in place through an inter-ministerial security committee and

---

[46] Marret, Jean-Luc. « L'organisation de la lutte antiterroriste en France », *Commentaires et forum*, Fondation pour la recherche stratégique, 17/09/2001.
http://www.frstrategie.org/version_fr/bandeau_FRS/archives/commentaires_forum/commentaires_forum71.asp?langue=fr

[47] Air France was the first carrier to install an "air marshal" plan post 9/11. A security agent was on board its first flight back to the U.S. on Friday, September 14, 2001 (Paris-Atlanta).
http://www.francetourism.com/update_Vigipirate.asp

endorsed by a bi-national Franco-British committee, the number of inspections has grown considerably since 11 Septemberth.

Internal Security Measures

The next wave of policies focused on internal physical security. This was achieved by increasing protection in public or other potential target areas (Vigipirate Renforcé Plan) and bolstering the authority of agencies fighting terrorist (Law on Everyday Security). Under the Loi sur la Sécurité Quotidienne, the following policies were enacted:

- Police and gendarmerie forces are authorised to inspect vehicles in the context of offences particularly damaging to public safety, e.g. terrorism;
- Unoccupied premises may be searched at night with a warrant from a magistrate in the context of offences relating to terrorism, the trafficking of arms, explosives or drugs;
- Video recordings may be made during interviews and videoconferencing technology may be used for witness confrontations for offences related to terrorism or drug trafficking;
- Personal files contained in police data-processing systems may be consulted by officials in the context of specific situations to be listed in a decree; and
- Measures to monitor email and Internet traffic are extended. Internet connection data and other technical data will be retained up to one year to permit identification and prosecution of offenders.

The objective of these policies is to improve situational awareness to prevent and pre-empt future terrorist attacks.

Measures Against Bio terrorism

Post 11 Septemberth, an epidemiological warning was issued requiring the mandatory notification and reporting of unusual phenomena such as anthrax (Plan Biotox). As part of the program, two military laboratories and a hospital were made available around the clock to facilitate microbiological diagnosis. Nine hospitals are currently assigned decontamination roles.

In addition, an evaluation was carried out to ascertain the availability of necessary medicines and vaccinations around hospitals and pharmaceutical laboratories. A specific inventory level is required and is currently being verified by authorities. To be on the safe side, the French government has placed an order worth 150 million Euro to ensure the availability of critical antibiotics[48]. A policy decision has also been made to increase vaccination stocks by three

---

[48] Such as BAL, Carbomix, Contrathion, Cyanokit and Kelocyanor

million to have a total of eight million doses. Finally, the government has taken measures to facilitate the provision of iodine tablets among the population.

Nuclear Protection

Historically, French nuclear plants have had limited protection against aircraft impacts. For example, safety rules providing guidance on the sizing of nuclear installations vis-à-vis the risk of aircraft impacts are over ten years old[49]. These rules stipulate that sizing decisions need to consider the potential impact of two types of aircraft: the Cessna 210 and the Learjet 23.

Post 11 September[th], additional measures were implemented to ensure the physical safety of vulnerable nuclear installations. On October 2001, the French Defence Ministry announced that radar systems capable of detecting low flying planes and air defence missiles had been deployed at La Hague and Il Longue[50]. Additional security measures introduced at nuclear facilities include further restriction of access to such facilities, improved surveillance of the facilities, and control of staff access to highly sensitive areas.

Conclusions

Overall, the measures taken by France post 9/11 represent a strong commitment to prevent and limit future terrorist attacks. The implementation of pre-existing anti-terrorist contingency plans (e.g. 'Vigipirate') to their highest level of alert has enhanced internal surveillance while giving law enforcement greater 'elbow room' to prevent future attacks. The French Federal Policy (Gendarmerie) operates at all levels and has therefore the position to provide oversight that is needed is terms of crisis. The creation of new committees (such as FINTER) has complemented the process by boosting coordination and information sharing among the large number of additional agencies involved in the fight against terrorism.

At the international level, France has renewed its commitment to greater information sharing at the European level. After the 11 September[th] attacks, French Minister of European Affairs Pierre Moscovici called for European nations to accelerate their judicial procedures and expand police cooperation in fighting terrorism. The French vision is to eventually have a European Justice system, a European police force, and European prosecutor's office to combat terrorism more efficiently.

---

[49] Règles fondamentales de sûreté (RFS) No.I.2a (August 1980) and No.I.1.a (September 1992). Source: World Information Service on Energy.

[50] La Hague is Europe's largest nuclear waste reprocessing plant. Il Longue is a military base for nuclear submarines off the Brittany coast in northwest France. Source: The Nuclear Age Peace Foundation.

Matrix of France's challenges, measures, actors, stages and progress

CHS: Challenges as outlined
Msrs: Measures 1-Strategic, 2-Operational, 3-Tactical
Actors: 1-Public sector, federal/national level, civil (including special forces), 2-Public sector, 3-Regional/state level, civil, 4-Public sector, local level, civil, 5-Military, 6-Private sector
Sgs: Stages: 1-pre-attack, 2-trans-attack, 3-post-attack
Pgs: Progress: 1-No specific post 9/11 action; 2-Need for action identified, policy in the making; 3-Budget appropriated, actors identified; 4-Policy implementation well underway; 5-Policy implementation finalised

Nr	Description France post 9/11 policymaking and -implementation	Categorisation				Remarks (budget in rounded figures)	Pgs
		Chs	Msrs	Ars	Sgs		
PREVENTION							
1	Greater information sharing between organizations involved in counter-terrorism	0	1	1	1-3	UCLAT	
	1. Expansion of interaction intelligence and security services						2
	2. Foster international cooperation					European Level	1
INFRASTRUCTURE PROTECTION							
2	Pre-established protection of critical infrastructures	0	3	1	1-3		
	1. Security enhancements at locations such as nuclear plants, large dams, and major industrial installations					More details under nuclear protection	4
SURVEILLANCE, SECURITISATION AND PUBLIC ORDER							
3	Additional measures for aviation safety	0	3	1	1	Goal: 100% check	
	1. Passengers and cabin baggage						5
	2. Luggage						5
	3. Personnel check						5
	4. Enhanced aircraft access control						4
	5. Improved methods for the inspection of freight and catering supplies						4
4	Securing internal borders and airspace	0	3	1,2,4	1-3		
	1. Reinforced air defence					La Hague plant	4
	3. Increased protection around US and Israeli embassies					Vigipirate	4
	4. Increased security along public transportation, tourist sites, places of worship, and other public areas					Vigipirate	4
	5. Expansion in number of law enforcement assets devoted to protection					Vigipirate: affects gendarmerie, national police	4
	6. Participation by military personnel in protection process					Approximately 1,000 personnel	4
5	Border control	0	1	1	1-3		
	1. Special security inspections of all Chunnel traffic					Includes passenger, tourist vehicle, trucking, and railway	4
TERRORISM AND NBC							
6	Protection against biological threats	4,6	3	1,4	2-3		
	1. Closer cooperation between civilian and military agencies					60 million euro	4
	2. Increased security at facilities for the production, storage, and transport of hazardous materials						4
	3. New agents of infectious disease added to list of poisonous substances					Biotox Plan	5
	4. Modified protocols for import					Biotox Plan	5
	5. Modified protocols for possession					Biotox	5
	6. Modified protocols for transfer					Biotox	5
	7. Modified protocols for acquisition					Biotox	5
	8. Modified protocols for transport					Biotox	5
	9. Designated hospitals and laboratories						5
	10. Inventory check (vaccinations)						4
	11. Availability of critical antibiotics					150 million euro	4
	12. Boost in inventory (vaccination)						4
	13. Iodine tablet distribution						4

	14. Mandatory reporting and notification of unusual biological phenomena						5
INTEGRITY FINANCIAL SECTOR AND COMBATING TERRORISM							
7	Greater Financial Surveillance	0	1,2	1	1		
	1. Creation of FINTER						
	2. New definitions in the area of financing terrorist activities						
	3. Additional penalties involving the confiscation of terrorist assets						
	4. Legal structure for the surveillance of money transfer offices						
	5. Enforcing the law on reporting unusual financial transactions and related news						
	6. Improved instruments to freeze suspicious accounts and transactions						
LEGAL ASPECTS							
8	Other internal security measures	0	2	1,2,3	1		
	1. Police authorization to inspect vehicles in context of offenses					Law on Everyday Security	4
	2. Gendarmerie authorization to inspect vehicles in context of offenses					Law on Everyday Security	4
	3. Search of unoccupied premises with a magistrate warrant					Law on Everyday Security	4
NUCLEAR PROTECTION							
9	Protection of nuclear sites	0	2	1	1		
	1. Air defence deployments					La Hague and Il Longue	5
	2. Installation of radar systems						5
	3. Further restriction of physical access to plants						4
	4. Control of staff access to highly sensitive areas						4
	5. Surveillance and overflight of facilities						4
TECHNOLOGICAL MEASURES							
10	Expansion in use of technological aides	0	2	1	1		
	1. Increased use of video-technology for witness confrontations					Law on Everyday Security	4
	2. Greater information access through data-processing systems					Law on Everyday Security	4
	3. Measures to expand monitoring of email and Internet traffic					Law on Everyday Security	4
EUROPEAN UNION							
11	Measures at European Union level	0	1,2	1	1		
	1. Asking for acceleration of judicial procedures					Ministry of Justice	1
	2. Asking for expanded police cooperation in fighting terrorism						1
OTHER							
12	International military operations	0	1	1,4	1,3		
	1. Participation in Operation Enduring Freedom						4

Germany

General overview

Background

The best-known example of 'recent' German terrorism is probably the RAF ('Rote Armee Fraction' -- Red Army Fraction). From 1960 on this proved to be a unique brand of German anti-establishment domestic terrorism that continued sporadically into the 1990s. In recent years there were incidents such as a police shoot-out with suspected RAF terrorist Wolfgang Grams, and the assassinations of prominent Germans.

Recent terrorism in Germany has not aimed at German targets. In a lot of other instances foreign targets were attacked, such as the 1986 bombing of the La Belle nightclub in Berlin that was frequented by U.S. soldiers stationed in the city. An earlier example is the deadly 1972 anti-Israeli terrorist attack at the Munich Olympics on 5 September 1972, when Palestinian Terrorists initially killed two Israeli athletes and took nine Israeli athletes hostage at the Olympic games in Munich, Germany, and the subsequent disaster when all athletes and terrorists, plus a German policeman, were killed in an effort to free the hostages.

Fig. 5. September 1972: the Olympic Flag lowered to half-mast in the Munich Olympic Stadium in memory of the 11 slain Israeli athletes

The attacks in Osnabrück in northern Germany are another example. In the last week of June 1996 suspected Irish Republican Army (IRA) terrorists left behind a three-meter-wide crater from an explosion directed at British soldiers and facilities in Osnabrück.

Reactions to 9/11

On 11 September, Chancellor Schröder called the Federal Security Council (Bundessicherheitsrat) together. The council met again on the 12th. That same day Chancellor Schröder came with an official government declaration. On the evening of the 12th, the Federal government approved the 'Bundnisfall'. The head of the Federal Chancellery (Bundeskanzleramte) established a security commission (Sicherheitslage) that meets every day. The task of this body, which comprises high-ranked representatives of the Foreign Office, Federal Ministry of Defence, Federal Ministry of the Interior, Federal Ministry of Justice, the Federal Chancellery and the German Intelligence Services ('der Deutschen

Dienste'), is to analyse actual and potential dangers for the Bundesrepublik Deutschland, to coordinate activities between the different authorities and to prepare the necessary measures and decisions. The German federal government offered the US-government support with regard to the consequences of the attacks.

Stronger security measures were taken with regard to the protection of Federal, US and Israeli facilities, transportation routes, airspace security and border control. Crisis management teams were formed in the Foreign Office and the Federal Ministry of the Interior and the amount of personnel in the centre of the Security commission (Lagezentrum) was raised. These three staffs held contact with each other and the Chancellor in an intensive way. The Foreign Office established an emergency phone number for relatives and provided security advice for travel to the US.

The security of the property and barracks of the army was raised. Stand-by mode ('Rufbereitschaft') and shift work were established, but not 'Alarmbereitschaft', neither vacation stops. A 'Bund-Länder' working group was established to study the effects on the security status. The German army offered the US every possible support.

A whole range of security measures was taken by the Minister of the Interior with regard to flights to the US, Israel and The UK. He also made an urgent request to the head of Air Traffic Control to undertake everything that is possible to guarantee an optimal management of starts and landings of aircraft. He assigned the Director of the Federal Agency of Aviation to the task of investigating in what way the created taskforce on Air Traffic Safety had checked aircraft on airfields.

Both the Chancellor and the head of the Federal Chancellery informed the chairmen of the fractions and parties on a regular basis. Because the PDS declared themselves against military involvement on October 6-7, secure information was withheld from that moment on.

On October 8, the government decided on an information centre for bio-warfare within the Robert Koch institute in Berlin. The tasks of this centre are: collecting information about biological weapons, analysing possible dangers and recommending solutions for better safety.

Some characteristics of the national institutional framework

The organigram below shows how subsets of Ministries form the National Security Commission, installed per 9/11, and the Federal Security Council, which has a permanent charactre. Also, there are separate crisis management teams in two ministries. Most of the relevant agencies are organised as part of the Ministry of the interior. This is a clear indication of the overall importance of this Ministry regarding the fight against terrorism.

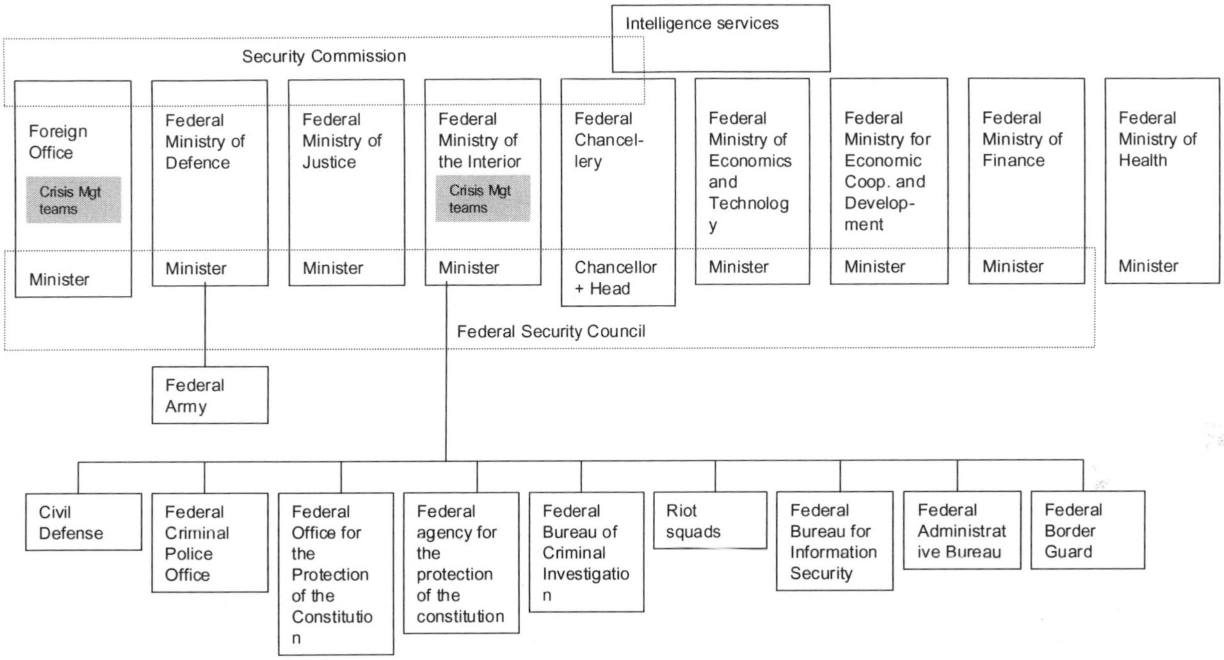

Figure 6. Organigram of relevant national actors for counter-terrorism in Germany

Even although some Ministries do not seem to be part of the Security Commission and -Council, they certainly play an important advisory role, such as the Ministry of Health.

Germany has a number of intelligence services that, according to our sources, work rather well together.

Selected elements of national policymaking and implementation

The various measures that have been taken in Germany as a response to the 9-11 attacks can be roughly divided into four categories:

1. Measures taken immediately after the 9-11 attacks
2. First counter-terrorism package

3. Second counter-terrorism package
4. Measures in particular targeted at financial aspects and money laundering

Measures taken immediately after the 9-11 attacks have been described in detail already in the previous section. Therefore we will focus here on both anti-terror packages and measures on money laundering.

Counter-terrorism packages and additional measures

On September 19, the Federal Government announced an additional budget for security measures in the year 2002 of approximately 1.5 billion Euro. The budget will be available through a 2 Eurocent increase on cigarette taxes and a 1-point percent increase on insurance taxes. The budget will be spent within the framework of two counter-terrorism packages, of which the first has been announced also on the 19th, and the second on 7 November. On November 30, the Upper House ('Bundesrat') agreed on the first package and on December 20, on the second package. Besides this, the government decided on additional measures in particular concerning the fight against terrorist organisations.

First package

The first anti-terror package, also called the '3 billion Mark program', sets an additional budget of 3 billion Mark for counter-terrorism measures. The budget will be divided across the different ministries as has been described earlier.

In the security area there is an additional budget of 700 mln. DM. This means a total of 2320 additional positions within the Federal Bureau of Criminal Investigation, Federal Agency for the Protection of the Constitution, Federal Border Guard and the Federal Bureau for Information Security. The first package focuses on both internal and external security, in addition to preventive actions concerning the 'roots' of terrorism. Half of the budget is targeted at the Federal Army ('Bundeswehr') and should make it possible to react in a flexible way at new conflict scenarios. The Federal Ministry of the Interior receives 100 mln Euro for improved border control, public safety ('Zivil- und Katastrophenschutz') and extra manpower/material for the Federal Criminal Police Office ('Bundeskriminalamt') and the Federal Office for the Protection of the Constitution ('Bundesamt für Verfassungsschutz). For both the Foreign Office and the Federal Ministry for Economic Cooperation and Development ('Bundesministerium für wirtschaftliche Zusammenarbeit'), there will be an additional budget of 100 mln Euro each, aimed at fighting the roots of terrorism and setting up international aid programs. The Federal Ministry of Justice and the Federal Ministry of Finance will receive 25 mln Euro (together) for investigational purposes and the fight against money laundering. The Federal Intelligence Service will also receive 25 mln Euro. The remaining 500 mln Euro will be put on reserve for addressing future developments.

On December 8, the Religion Privileges were discarded, which means that it is possible to prohibit organisations that use religious practice as cover for extremist aims. Also, a change was made in the Penal Code, which makes it possible not only to penalize members of criminal or terrorist organisations based in Germany, but also members of such organizations based in other countries.

Federal Border Guard

For the Federal Border Guard, this means an additional budget of 120 mln Euro, 1.450 additional positions for police wards, 50 positions for IT-personnel and 470 administrative positions. Part of the budget will be used for establishing a new section within the Federal Border Guard for employment of about 200 Sky Marshalls (Flugsicherheitsbegleiter). Besides this the budget will be used for object- and personnel related security measures (also for German offices abroad), strengthening of information- and communication technology within the Federal Border Guard, in the 'Dokumentenprüftechnik' and in the improvement of the ABC-emergency service ('ABC-Einsatzdienste').

Federal Bureau of Criminal Investigation (Bundeskriminalamt)

The Federal Bureau of Criminal Investigation receives an additional budget of 40 mln Euro. This means 244 additional positions for security of persons ('Personenschutz'), investigation/ analysis/ evaluation, the technical-scientific area and Europol. The areas of 'Kriminaltechnik', communication and logistics will be strengthened in addition to a Central Bureau for Money Laundering.

Federal agency for the protection of the constitution (Bundesamt für Verfassungsschutz)

The Federal agency for the protection of the constitution receives an additional budget of 10 mln Euro for strengthening its observation of terrorist activities in the areas of alien extremism, Federal terrorism and proliferation.

Federal Bureau for Information Security

The Federal Bureau for Information Security receives an additional budget of 15 mln Euro and 21 positions.

Riot squads (Bereitschaftspolizeien)

There is an additional budget of 14 mln Euro for the various riot squads on the regional ('Länder') level. This budget will be used for:

Emergency vehicles

Photo/video equipment

Body protection outfits

Federal Administrative Bureau (Bundesverwaltungsamt)

The Federal Administrative Bureau will receive 9 mln Euro for 44 additional positions. The budget will be used for technical support, the Central Alien Registry, Visa and IT-security.

Civil defense (Zivilschutz)

The Civil Defence receives 13 mln Euro for the establishment of a central information centre for crisis situations. Furthermore the budget will be used for NBC-exploratory and -decontamination vehicles, ambulance services and 'Betreeungsfahrzeuge', a better communication system (radio, telephone). The 'Akademie für Notfallplanung und Zivilschutz' will be strengthened and developed into a 'Kompetenzzentrum für Bund-Länder-Krisenmanagement'.

Second package

The second package basically means the establishment of a new German law, aimed at the fight against terrorism ('Terrorismusbekämpfungsgesetz'). This *New Terrorism* act is effective since January 1, 2002. Within this new law there is range of adjustments to other related laws. The new law aims at:

- Providing the authorities with the right legal competence
- Improving the required information exchange between authorities
- Prevent the entrance of terrorist criminals in Germany
- Improve identity checking within visa procedures
- Giving the opportunity of employing armed air guards on German aircraft
- Improving border control
- Improving knowledge of extremists already staying in Germany

This in addition to more practical measures, such as:

- Making it possible to perform security checks for employees in essential facilities
- Making it possible to incorporate biometric characteristics in identity cards
- Reserving weapons for the use by policemen in civil aircraft
- Making it possible to prevent activities of extremist foreign organisations
- Making computerized searches ('Rasterfahndung') more effective by combining several databases with civil information
- Securing energy provision

Within the framework of the anti-terror act there have been changes to the following acts:

- Act on the Protection of the Constitution (Bundesverfassungsschutzgesetz)
- Military Intelligence Service Act (Gesetz über den Militärischen Abschirmdienst – MAD-gesetz)
- Federal Intelligence Service Act (Gesetz über den Bundesnachrichtendienst – BND-Gesetz)

- Federal Border Guard Act (Bundesgrenzschutzgesetz)
- Federal Bureau of Criminal Investigation Act (Bundeskriminalamtgesetz)
- Aliens Act (Ausländergesetz)
- Asylum Procedure Act (Asylverfahrensgesetz)
- Alien Central Registry Act (Ausländerzentralregistergesetzes)
- Act on Security Clearance Checks (Sicherheitsüberprüfungsgesetz)
- Passport Act (Passgesetz)
- Act on Identity cards (Gesetz über Personalausweise)
- Organization law (Vereinsgesetz)
- Air Traffic Act (Luftverkehrsgesetz)
- Federal Central Register Act (Bundeszentralregistergesetz)
- Tenth book of the Social Security Code (Sozialgesetzbuchs)
- Act on Energy Security

Act on the Protection of the Constitution (Bundesverfassungsschutzgesetz)

The federal agency for the protection of the constitution has the right to observe attempts against the ideas of the understanding among nations or against the peaceful living together of nations. This right is already incorporated in several regional (Länder)-level Acts on the Protection of the Constitution. In order to investigate money streams (linked to possible terrorist persons or organizations) the federal agency for the constitution has the right to collect information on bank accounts at banks and other financial institutions. They also have this right with regard to postal services, air traffic organizations and telecommunication services.

Federal Bureau of Criminal Investigation Act (Bundeskriminalamtgesetz)

In certain unusual heavy appearances of cyber crime, the Federal Bureau of Criminal Investigation has the authority to start the prosecution without being asked or ordered to do so. The competences of the headquarters of the Bureau will be strengthened, and certain bureaucratic obstacles will be removed. This should lead to a better information procurement by collecting facts and performing analysis.

Federal Border Guard Act

The employment of security personnel (Flugsicherheitsbegleiter) on board of German airplanes is now regulated. Furthermore it is possible for the Federal Border Guards not only to stop and interrogate persons, but also to screen their travel documents extensively. Other new measures include a better information exchange, prohibition of the entry of terrorist offenders to Germany and the necessary security measures with regard to identification.

Aliens Act (Ausländergesetz)

The changes in the aliens act will lead to a situation wherein a certain category of people will no longer get a visa or residence permit. This category consists of people who are a danger to the liberal democratic basis of Germany or to the German Bundesrepublik, who are themselves engaged or who encourage others to engage in violence in order to reach their political objectives or who belong to an organisation that sustains international terrorism.

The changes in the Aliens Act also lead to a basis for more intensive cooperation between agencies abroad and security authorities. There were also more extensive ways of identity checks, in particular in agencies abroad with regard to visa. Finally, the changes in the Aliens Act provided inter-state regulations with on machine-readable areas for the 'EU-Aufenthaltstitel'. The establishment of forgery-proof identity cards was extended to asylum-seekers and 'Duldungsinhaber'.

Asylum Procedure Act (Asylverfahrensgesetz)

In the Asylum Procedure Act there is a new legal basis for speech recording. With the analysis of this identity securing speech record, the region of origin can be determined. Fingerprints and other information won with regard to an asylum procedure will be stored for 10 years. The changes in this act will also make it possible to make an automatic comparison between fingerprints of asylum-seekers and databases of the Federal Bureau of Criminal Investigation.

Alien Central Registry Act (Ausländerzentralregistergesetzes)

Important changes in the Alien Central Registry Act made it possible to get more data out of the Alien Central Registry (Ausländerzentralregister). The visa registry was extended to a visa decision-registry, with an enhanced access for police authorities. The security services now have access to these electronic databases in a continuous way.

Act on Security Clearance Checks (Sicherheitsüberprüfungsgesetz)

Changes in the Act on Security Clearance Checks mean that employees who (will) work in important health or defence facilities will undergo security checks.

Air Traffic Act (Luftverkehrsgesetz)

Within the Air Traffic Act there now is a phrase that states that the use of guns on board a civil airplane is reserved for police wards, in particular to the Federal Border Control. Reliability tests of employees at airports and air traffic business now have a better regulation in the air traffic act.

Passport Act (Passgesetz) and Act on Identity cards (Gesetz über Personalausweise)

Within the framework of these two acts there have been improvements in the possibilities of computer-based identification of persons. Besides the photo and signature there will be an additional biometric characteristic in the passport and identity card. The practical matters of this will be regulated in an additional 'Bundesgesetz'.

Organization law (Vereinsgesetz)

Within organisation law the 'religionsprivilege' was abandoned and it now became possible to prohibit the support of foreign terrorist organisations by people in Germany. Showing symbols of prohibited organisations is also forbidden.

Money Laundering

After the 9-11 attacks there have been two major efforts in Germany to combat money laundering and ensure stable financial markets. First, there has been a range of measures within the framework of a Fourth Financial Market Promotion Act, which will be effective from the 1st of July this year. Second, the Act on the Track Down of Profits from Heavy Crimes ('Gesetzes über das Aufspüren von Gewinnen aus schweren Straftaten'), will be changed into a Money Laundering Act ('Geldwäschebekämpfungsgesetz').

Measures within the framework of a Fourth Financial Market Promotion Act[51]

The tightening of checks on the ownership of banks and insurance companies is intended to prevent the acquisition of a substantial participation in a bank, financial services provider or insurance undertaking being obtained with funds deriving from illegal activity. This will counter the risk of the funds put into such undertakings being laundered as a result of the acquisition or the undertaking being used for further money laundering operations.

Credit institutions will be required to set up adequate internal systems to protect against money laundering and financial fraud both in wholesale and especially in retail business, using EDP. This is to allow business transactions to be screened for risk groups and conspicuous features. It will also enable existing gaps in customer identification to be closed in the case of specific contractual financial services transactions.

Undertakings carrying on credit card business will in future require a license to do so and will be subject to ongoing supervision by the Federal Banking Supervisory Office (BAKred). Credit card business, which has not hitherto been supervised, is being increasingly abused for money laundering operations. The ongoing supervision of such undertakings is intended to ensure compliance with anti-money-laundering standards in this field of business.

Installation of a bank account information exchange. A central database is to be installed at the BAKred in which banks will be required to place information on all accounts and securities accounts held in Germany. This measure is to assist in revealing money flows in support of

[51] The text of this section has been derived from a press background paper of the German Federal Ministry of Finance. http://www.bundesfinanzministerium.de/Anlage7860/Uebersetzung-in-Englisch.pdf

terrorism and money laundering and to help counter unlicensed banking business and underground banking. It will do away with the current need to address enquiries to some 2,900 institutions. The amendments to the Fiscal Code and the Income Tax Law are intended to ensure that facts discovered by the revenue authorities in exercising their supervisory function that indicate money laundering or comparable offences can be passed on to the law enforcement authorities.

To make anti-money-laundering measures more effective, a "Central Financial Intelligence Unit" will also be set up within the sphere of activity of the Federal Ministry of Finance. The tasks of this FIU will be:

- The central FIU receives all notifications of suspected money laundering made in the country as a whole.
- The central FIU analyses and evaluates the suspicious transaction notifications before passing them on (if the suspicion is substantiated) together with additional facts to the investigating authorities (public prosecutors' offices). The central FIU is organized so as to provide an information pool on suspected money laundering and a centralized jurisdiction, and is staffed with personnel from a range of disciplines. It brings together the professional knowledge and experience of customs officers, financial market supervisors, law enforcement officers, public accountants, and bankers.
- Outside of legal assistance procedure the central FIU provides a single contact point to ensure international cooperation in countering money laundering in administrative procedure with other FIUs and exchanges information relating to money laundering in advance of the institution of investigative proceedings.
- The central FIU prepares background reports on the handling of specific matters and procedures and situation reports on money laundering methods and types in a specific country which are passed on to the reporting institutions to assist them in identifying money laundering operations in business practice.

A further package of measures is intended to ensure the security and stability of financial markets as a protection against terrorist infiltration. The following action will be taken within the framework of the Fourth Financial Market Promotion Act:

- Enhancing the range of instruments for detecting insider trading by extending the supervisory powers of the Federal Securities Supervisory Office (BAWe).
- Extending the supervision of reinsurance companies by the Federal Insurance Supervisory Office.

Further measures are planned which may be incorporated in the Fourth Financial Market Promotion Act. These involve the following proposals for regulation:

- Introduction of a provision empowering the BAWe to impose in difficult market situations a ban or volume restriction on all short selling.
- Extending the reporting requirements set out in section 9 of the Securities Trading Act to include security-based repurchase agreements and securities lending transactions. This will firstly create the necessary transparency. Secondly, it will make available to the BAWe information on the positions held. Together with the information on short sales the BAWe will thus be supplied with the data enabling it to intervene in times of crisis. Moreover, these data can be used for the detection and prosecution of insider trading offences.
- Granting the BAWe powers to access the lending data accumulated in connection with security-based repurchase agreements and securities lending transactions at banks and clearing houses (holding before and after the transaction, borrower and lender). Where transactions are settled through clearing houses in other European countries, the BAWe must be empowered to issue cross-border requests for information. In this respect there is a need for a uniform, Europe-wide approach.

Money Laundering Act[52]

With the money Laundering Act there will be stronger measures regarding identification and notification by suspicious transactions. The Money Laundering Act will be updated with regard to electronic media. Software based research and monitoring systems should lead to the tracking of money laundering.

Furthermore the Money Laundering Act implements two important international directives: The second European directive[53] on Money Laundering and the recommendations of the FATF (Financial Action Task Force)[54].

Germany in an international context

On an international level Germany has held talks regarding terrorism with a range of other countries. On September 19, Schröder and British Prime-Minister Blair together made a condemning statement against terrorism. On September 20, there were talks between NATO secretary-general George Robertson and the Chancellor of Germany. On September 21/22 the German Foreign Minister visited President Bush and UN secretary-general Annan. A few days later on the 25th, Putin visited Chancellor Schröder in Berlin. On October 2, Foreign Minister Joschka Fischer visited Syrian President Bashar al-Assad and Foreign Minister

[52] See: 'Entwurf eines Gesetzes zur Verbesserung der Bekämpfung der Geldwäsche und der Bekämpfung der Finanzierung des Terrorismus (Geldwäschebekämpfungsgesetz)' http://www.bmi.bund.de/Annex/de_20067/Entwurf_eines_Geldwaeschebekaempfungsgesetzes.pdf

[53] Richtlijn 2001/97/EG van het Europees Parlement en de Raad tot wijziging van Richtlijn 91/308/EEG van de Raad tot voorkoming van het gebruik van het financiële stelsel voor het witwassen van geld

[54] See: Financial Action Task Force on Money Laundering, *The fourty recommendations.* http://www1.oecd.org/fatf/40Recs_en.htm

FarThe UK el-Shara. That same day he spoke in Beirut to Prime-minister Rafik Hariri, foreign minister Mahmud Hammud and head of parliament Nabih Berri. Besides the connections within the European Union, there were also visits on the political level to New York, Washington, Pakistan, India, China, the Middle East and Russia.

Germany received considerable international attention by hosting the Afghanistan conference in Bonn, November 27 till December 5. One of the most debated issues in Germany was the involvement of German soldiers in foreign countries, as would be the case with Afghanistan. On December 22, the Parliament agreed on this involvement, and on January 11 the first German troops arrived in Afghanistan. This was the first time after WWII that German soldiers engaged in foreign combat.

Conclusion

Germany has thoroughly crafted new legislation to identify terrorism and to be able to proactively monitor and prosecute terrorists or persons and organisations that support terrorists. The issue of 'rasterfahndung', which is the ability to intelligently search different databases, may be rather unique to Germany. In addition, Germany is embarking on a program that may lead to improved accessibility to biometry, in particular fingerprints. Germany has also created impressive budgets to strengthen various institutions of the federal government. In particular, Germany has undertaken to create a solid financial monitoring approach within the appropriate legal structure to cut the ties between terrorism and financing. Finally, Germany has been remarkably active in the international arena from hosting the Future-of-Afghanistan conference to military engagement.

Matrix of Germany's challenges, measures, actors, stages and progress

CHS: Challenges as outlined
Msrs: Measures 1-Strategic, 2-Operational, 3-Tactical
Actors: 1-Public sector, federal/national level, civil (including special forces), 2-Public sector, 3-Regional/state level, civil, 4-Public sector, local level, civil, 5-Military, 6-Private sector
Sgs: Stages: 1-pre-attack, 2-trans-attack, 3-post-attack
Pgs: Progress: 1-No specific post 9/11 action; 2-Need for action identified, policy in the making; 3-Budget appropriated, actors identified; 4-Policy implementation well underway; 5-Policy implementation finalised

Nr	Description Germany post 9/11 policymaking and -implementation	Categorisation				Remarks (budgets in rounded figures kEuro per year)	Pgs
		Chs	Mrs	Ars	Sgs		
	ACTIONS IMMEDIATELY FOLLOWING 9/11 ATTACKS						
1	Establishment of a security commission (Sicherheitslage)	1-6	2-3	1	1-3	comprises high-ranked representatives of the Foreign Office, Federal Ministry of Defense, Federal Ministry of the Interior, Federal Ministry of Justice, the Federal Chancellery and the German Intelligence Services	
2	Stronger security measures taken immediately after 9/11	1-6	3	1,2 3,5	1-2		
	1. protection of Federal, US and Israel facilities						
	2. protection of transportation routes						
	3. improved airspace security						
	4. improved border control						
3	Forming of Crisis management teams	1-6	2	1	1-2	in the Foreign Office and the Federal Ministry of the Interior	
4	Establishment of an emergency phone number for relatives	3-4	3	1	3	In the Foreign Office	
5	Army on Stand-by mode (Rufbereitschaft) and shift work	3-6	3	4	1-2		
6	A 'Bund-Länder' working group was established to study the effects on the security status	1-6	2	1-2	1-3		
7	Security measures with regard to flights to the US, Israel and The UK.	3-6	3	1,5	1-2	taken by the Minister of the Interior	
	1. Putting down airplanes on specific security positions						
	2. Entrance checks on put down airplanes by specific official security staff						
	3. Escort of airplanes on the airport by motorised security staff						
	4. Inspection of persons who are permitted entrance and the objects they carry by security staff						
	5. Observation of put down airplanes by security staff						
	6. Inspection of approach busses before travellers attend						
	7. Observation of terminals by armed security staff						
	8. Escort of travellers by security staff from and to airplanes						
	9. Securing of check-in by armed security staff						
	10. Complete manual, bodily inspection of travellers, technical equipment may only be used as additional equipment						
	11. Complete inspection of hand luggage, technical equipment may only be used as additional equipment						
	12. Secure observation and complete inspection of luggage by technical equipment						
8	Establishment of information center for bio warfare	2,4, 6	1	1,5	1-3	within the Robert Koch institute in Berlin	
	1. collecting information about biological						

	weapons						
	2. analysing possible dangers						
	3. recommending solutions for better safety						
FIRST ANTI-TERROR PACKAGE							
9	Improved flexibility for army reactions on new conflicts	1-6	1	1,4	2	0,7 bln Euro (Federal Army)	
10	Measures taken by Ministry of Interior	1-6	1	1		250 mln Euro (Ministry of Interior)	
	1. Operational ability of Federal Border Guard strengthened						
	2. Operational ability of Federal Criminal Justice Office strengthened						
	3. Federal agency for the protection of the Constitution strengthened						
11	Measures taken by Foreign Office and Ministry for Economic cooperation	1-6	1	1		100 mln. Euro each (Foreign Office and Bundesministerium für wirtschaftliche Zusammenarbeit)	
	1. Fighting the roots of terrorism						
	2. Aid programs for affected regions						
	3. Caring for refugees						
	4. Strengthening of intercultural dialog						
12	Measures taken by Ministry of Justice and Ministry of Finance	1-6	1	1		25 mln. Euro together (Ministry of Justice and Ministry of Finance)	
13	Measures taken by Federal Intelligence Service	1-6	1	1		25 mln. Euro	
14	Religion Privileges were discarded	1-6	1	1		This means that it is possible to prohibit organizations that use religious practice as cover for extremist aims.	
15	Change in the Penal Code	1-6	1	1		This makes it possible not only to penalize members of criminal or terrorist organizations based in Germany, but also members of such organizations based in other countries.	
SECOND ANTI-TERROR PACKAGE							
16	Providing the authorities with the right legal competence	1-6	2	1-3	1		
17	Improving the required information exchange between authorities	1-6	2	1-3	1		
18	Prevent the entrance of terrorist criminals in Germany	1-6	2	1-3	1		
19	Improve identity checking within visa procedures	1-6	2	1-3	1		
20	Giving the opportunity of employing armed air guards on German aircraft	1-6	2	4	1		
21	Improving border control	1-6	2	1-2	1		
22	Improving knowledge of extremists already staying in Germany	1-6	2	1	1		
23	Making it possible to perform security checks for employees in essential facilities	1-6	2	1-3,5	1		
24	Making it possible to incorporate biometric characteristics in identity cards	1-6	2	1-3,5	1		
25	Reserving weapons for the use by policemen in civil aircraft	1-6	3	1-3	1-2		
26	Making it possible to prevent activities of extremist foreign organizations	1-6	2	1	1		
27	Making computerized searches ('Rasterfahndung') more effective by combining several databases with civil information	1-6	2	1	1		
28	Securing energy provision	5	3	1	2-3		
MONEY LAUNDERING							
29	Fourth Financial Market Promotion Act	1-6	1-2	1-5	1		
	1. Supervision of credit card business and Tightening of checks on origins of money flows						
	2. Amendments to fiscal code and income tax law: Banks have the duty to investigate and report suspicious transactions, need for organizational measures and improved information systems						
	3. Establishment of a specific bank account database, with data of all clients of Germany's 3000 banks						

30	Revision of Money Laundry Act of 1993	1-6	1-2	1-5	1		
	1. Implementation of 2nd EU directive on money laundry5. Expansion public prosecution offices						
	2. Implementation of 8th recommendation of FETF						
31	Establishment of Financial Intelligence Unit within Federal Investigation Bureau in Wiesbaden	1-6	1-2	1-5	1		

Netherlands

General overview

Background

The Netherlands has limited experience with homeland acts of terrorism over the last few decades. In February 1973 a close combat response team was formed ('Bijzondere Bijstands Eenheid, BBE') in response to the tragic events in Munich, Germany.

The BBE has since been active in a small number of cases, most notably the hijacking on 2 December 1975 of a train, by terrorists demanding a free republic of the 'Molluken' (South-East Indonesia, in particular Ambon). Two passengers and the conductor were killed. On 23 May 1977, members of the same terrorist group again hijacked a train with over two hundred passengers but also at the same time an elementary school, taking about one hundred children and five teachers hostage.

Fig 7. May 1977: Terrorists release sick children and teachers from the elementary school they have seized in Bovensmilde.

The terrorists demanded the release of their imprisoned brothers that conducted the previous train hijacking and others who had been responsible for the occupation of the Indonesian consulate, an event that happened in 1975. The school situation was resolved within a few days, primarily because the children and teachers got ill[55], but the train hijacking was ended by the BBE, killing only two passengers, in an action that is still being used worldwide as a teaching example for counter terrorist action today.

The Netherlands may be particularly sensitive to international terrorism for three reasons[56]:

- Geographically, The Netherlands is an important node in international flows of goods, persons and intangibles, most notably through its mainport of Schiphol airport and Rotterdam Harbour, which are as large as the largest international mainports and are therefore very large relative to the size of the country.
- Internationally, The Netherlands is home to the following organisations that may attract terrorists: The International Court of Law; The Yugoslavia Tribunal; the OPCW

[55] Some say authorities poisoned the childrens' and teachers' food on purpose

[56] 'Terrorism at the beginning of the 21st century. Threat analysis and positioning of the AIVD'. AIVD, Leidschendam, April 2001 (in Dutch)

(the UN organisation for inspection of chemical weapons proliferation) and the Lockerbie process.

- In terms of migration, The Netherlands has lately seen large influxes of refugees and other immigrants that may have connections with or sympathy for terrorists or their causes.
- The Netherlands is known to be tolerant, both in daily life in society as well as with respect to prosecution and punishment

Most recently, on September 27, 2001, the BBE was involved in a bomb scare concerning four major tunnels in the Amsterdam and Rotterdam areas. At the request of the Ministers of the Interior and Justice, the Police, the Royal Netherlands Military Constabulary and BBE together secured the tunnels and checked all traffic. Dutch airspace was closed for a short period. There were no signs of terrorists detected. The public prosecutor has recently (April 2002) discontinued the search for the perpetrator(s).

The Dutch government recognised early on that the root for the Molukkan terrorist actions was the Dutch colonial past, and, more specifically, the fact that this past had not been publicly and correctly dealt with. As a result, national policies were formulated and implemented to engage in discussions with Molukkans and other minority groups. This approach, to include all stakeholders in public dialogue and consensus building (some call it the 'polder model') may have prevented new terrorist actions. However, another explanation may be that the terrorist actions were not appreciated in the Molukkan community in The Netherlands itself; this community in general respects authority and opposes acts of violence.

Monitoring domestic groups that may be prone to perform terrorist activities, such as radical or extreme elements within certain communities, and to a lesser extent extreme individuals, is something that Dutch intelligence has taken care of rather well. The three main intelligence units in The Netherlands are civil intelligence BVD[57]), military intelligence (MID) and Joint national police research intelligence (CRI -KLPD). Although these are separate entities, they work together quite well whenever this is deemed necessary. In addition, they have their internationals counterparts with whom they cooperate, providing a tight international intelligence network, both in Europe as well as beyond Europe.

A number of recent major disasters, such as an El-Al airplane crash on a suburb of Amsterdam (1992; 52 fatalities) and a massive fireworks explosion in the city of Enschede (2000; 20 dead, 200 injured) have drummed up both awareness and policymaking with respect to capabilities of first responders as well as general perspectives on how to deal with national security, including prioritising risks, cost-benefit analyses of prevention and risk

[57] The BVD (Domestic Security Service) just recently changed its name into AIVD (General Intelligence and Security Service) thus reflecting the institutional response to the changing threat scenario.

management, disaster and consequence management and many other related issues. Some say that even the Dutch experience in Srebrenica in 1995, where the military witnessed probably the most extreme act of terrorism – genocide – has had its influence at all relevant levels in Dutch society, from soldiers to politicians, namely that unimaginable acts of terrorism are possible, and that the fight against terrorism therefore requires a vast spectrum of measures that are all interlinked, from proper equipment and outfitting, to trained personnel and clear lines of command, control, responsibility and authority.

Terrorism is yet undefined in Dutch legislation and terrorists are therefore prosecuted as violent criminals, leading to relatively less severe punishment than they would receive in many other European countries. New laws are in the making to address the latter issue and to harmonize the situation relative to other countries in accordance with recent European resolutions[58]. The Netherlands however is careful labelling violent acts not too quickly as 'terrorist' acts, because in doing so, the state may 'declare war' on groups with violent activities and thus block the reintegration of such groups into society. An example of this position was the strategy that was taken towards the violent action group RaRa that bombed and set on fire various buildings in the period 1985 – 1993[59].

Also, there remains a gap in The Netherlands between the identification of individuals and groups that are prone to committing acts of terrorism (including threats), and individuals or groups actually carrying out these acts. The latter group can be prosecuted, but the former can to a certain extent only be monitored. This 'gap' worries some high level national policymakers, and it may become a focus of future policymaking.

Reactions to 9/11[60]

Following the attacks in the United States, The Netherlands government has been giving even more priority to combating terrorism than before. On 18 September, a ministerial steering committee ('stuurgroep') was established consisting of the Prime Minister (chairman) and the Ministers of Justice, Interior, Defence, Finance, Transport and Foreign affairs, plus both vice-prime ministers, i.e. the Ministers of Health and Economic Affairs. The Ministerial committee was supported by an interdepartmental commission at the level of Directors General, and by an interdepartmental task force, led by the Director General for Law enforcement of the Ministry of Justice. Individual Ministers were supported by Ministerial task forces, most notably the Minister of Defence and the Minister of the Interior, in particular on NBC related issues and health emergency response.

---

[58] Legislation has been drafted in The Netherlands that recognises membership of a criminal organisation with a terrorist goal. The draft is currently under consideration by the Council of State

[59] 'Terrorism at the beginning of the 21st century. Threat analysis and positioning of the AIVD'. AIVD, Leidschendam, April 2001 (in Dutch)

[60] Much of this text originates from the press release of the Ministerial Council 0826 at www.minjus.nl

The committee and interdepartmental task force quickly put together an action plan for combating terrorism and promoting security that contains a package of measures with which the government wishes to step up anti- and counter-terrorism. It was first published on 5 October and communicated to the House of Representatives. It has been continuously updated since, while the focus evolved from policymaking to policy implementation. The action plan concerns both the reinforcement of existing policy and new emphasis and priorities[61].

There will be no major structural changes in responsibilities and authority. The initiatives focus on prevention as well as expeditious investigation and successful prosecution of terrorist crimes. According to an initial and rough estimate, the extra measures would involve a budget of up to 100 million Euro annually. In a separate document of the task force on defence and terrorism, published in January 2002, it was also concluded that the mission of the military should remain unchanged in light of 9/11, but that certain military institutions and tasks should be strengthened, such as special forces, NBC response capabilities and intelligence.

Clearly, The Netherlands Government supports the vision that international terrorism can only be fought with an international coalition. It has therefore actively participated in UN, NATO and EU negotiations, resolutions and initiatives to harmonise policymaking, policy implementation and operational activities where appropriate (such as freezing assets and prosecuting terrorism suspects). Also, the bilateral negotiations with the USA following 9/11 were of great importance, both at the strategic level, such as acknowledgement – albeit hesitantly and with heated internal discussions – of the issue of 'war against terrorism', as well as the operational level, such as acting upon the receipt of US lists of suspected persons and organisations.

Domestically, direct measures were taken to improve information sharing between relevant parties, in particular military and non-military intelligence (MID and AIVD). The AIVD works closely with European and non-European sister organizations, including the FBI. AIVD was put on a higher status of alert and daily threat analyses were issued by the AIVD together with TEC, the Technical Evaluation Committee. These analyses were discussed in the so-called evaluation triangle ('evaluatie driehoek'), involving representatives of the Ministries of the Interior and Justice and the AIVD, plus advisory members of Defence and Foreign Affairs. The Council of Police Chiefs (RHC), in addition, has issued scenarios to assist the work of the evaluation triangle and to help the Minister of the Interior to determine to what extent BBE's services can be called upon.

---

[61] A confidential version of the action plan also exists

Some characteristics of the national institutional framework

Below is a simple diagram that explains the cabinet- and interdepartmental crisis response policy configuration relating to terrorist attacks (and other disastrous events):

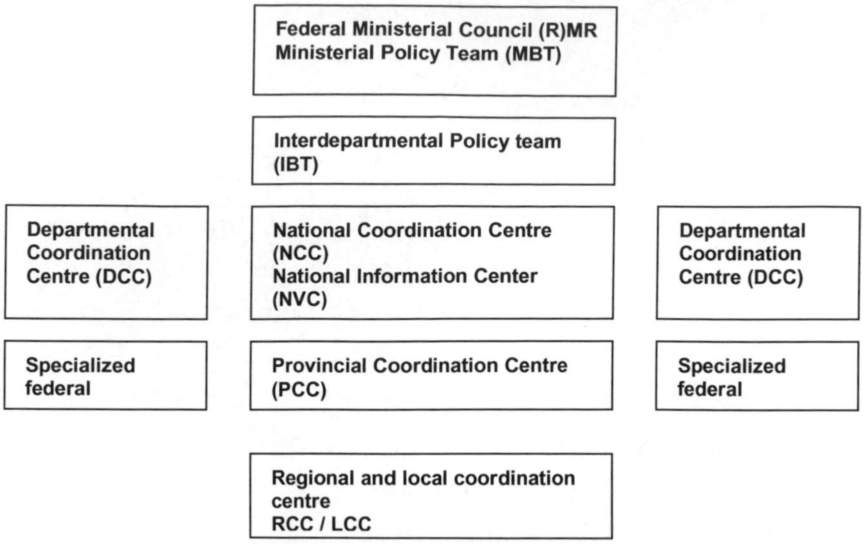

Fig. 8 Diagram depicting the cabinet- and interdepartmental crisis response policy configuration.

There is not one centralized specific responsibility and authority for combating terrorism in The Netherlands. Terrorism is covered within the existing structures. It is argued that any act of terrorism, be it a threat or an actual attack, is always punishable by criminal law. And any act against criminals is the responsibility of the Ministry of Justice. Therefore, the Minister of Justice is usually in the leading position, in particular when swift response is necessary. Other Ministries are expected to provide support, and therefore have the responsibility to have the supporting structures and services in place. For homeland response to non-criminal disasters, the Ministry of the Interior has the lead as it has in maintaining public order, for instance related to soccer games. Other Ministries, including the Ministry of Defence, the Ministry of Health and the Ministry of Environment, act in support of the Ministry of Justice and the Ministry of the Interior, but also have their own responsibilities. For crisis situations, procedures for departmental, interdepartmental and ministerial policy and decision-making as well as communication at federal, provincial and local level are well established. In fact, detailed cabinet- and interdepartmental crisis response policy configurations have been established for six different crises:

- Military and international political crises
- Terrorism
- Nuclear disaster
- Oil crisis
- North Sea disasters

- Extended crises, involving a number of the above

In the House of Representatives, questions have been asked after 9/11 suggesting the centralisation of Homeland Defence against terrorism such as in the USA, where the Office of Homeland Defence has been put into place. The Dutch government has responded negatively to these suggestions, saying it would disrupt the existing structures that seem - and have been proven - to work well.

Having said that, it is interesting to notice that the closure of airspace following the bomb scare on September 27th 2001 indicated that the final authority for doing so lies with the Minister of Transport, which differs from the Minister of Justice being able to 'tell' the Minister of Transport to provide support by closing the airspace. In other words, there was confusion about airspace closure because the divisions of responsibility and authority were not completely clear, or so it seemed to turn out in practice. Thus, although the response structure overall is well defined in The Netherlands, some specific elements of response may benefit from even better definition, leaving less room for difference in interpretation regarding authority and responsibility. In this respect, there may be a need to better define the supporting role of Defence as well, even although is has been concluded that the general mission of the military will remain unchanged. This may be another area for future policymaking, in addition to the 'gap' identified earlier. Just recently, a Defence review indicated that there is a need to overhaul the top command and control structure. In the course of negotiating this review, terrorism related issues, such as providing support to homeland defence, might be considered as well.

Another interesting point to note is that, like in many other countries, The Netherlands realizes that first response to threats and attacks will always be local. Hence the name first responders or local responders. No matter what the threat or attack, local responders will see to it first. The responsibility is therefore also local, i.e. lies with the Mayor. The leading role for instance of the Mayor of Enschede concerning the firework blast mentioned earlier, compares well, albeit on a smaller scale, with the leading role of the mayor of New York in the case of 9/11. In The Netherlands, local and national parties have structured their information exchange in the triangle mentioned earlier. The "Federal Triangle' consists of three corners. In the top corner we find mainly the Minister of Justice. In the second corner we find the Minister of the Interior. In the third corner the main position is for the Director of the Civil Intelligence Service (AIVD). Other ministries, most notably Defence and Foreign Affairs have an advisory role.

At the local level, we find similar triangles of information exchange and decision-making. Locally, the Mayor is in the top corner, as stated above. Other corners of the triangle are occupied by Chief Justice Officers (of 19 regions) and local Chiefs of Police.

The relationship between the federal triangle and the local triangles is advisory. There are no 'direct lines of command'. For example, although the bomb threat of 27 September to Rotterdam and Amsterdam tunnels was identical, the local response was set up according to local decision making and local context and was therefore (slightly) different.

The National Coordination Centre (NCC) has the responsibility for undisrupted and secure information exchange regarding the response to terrorist attacks between federal, provincial, regional and local authorities. The National Information Centre (NVC) will take care of the provision of information to the general public, combining all information of public institutions.

The next organigram shows relations between political decision-making, governmental bodies and operational organisation relating to counter-terrorism in The Netherlands

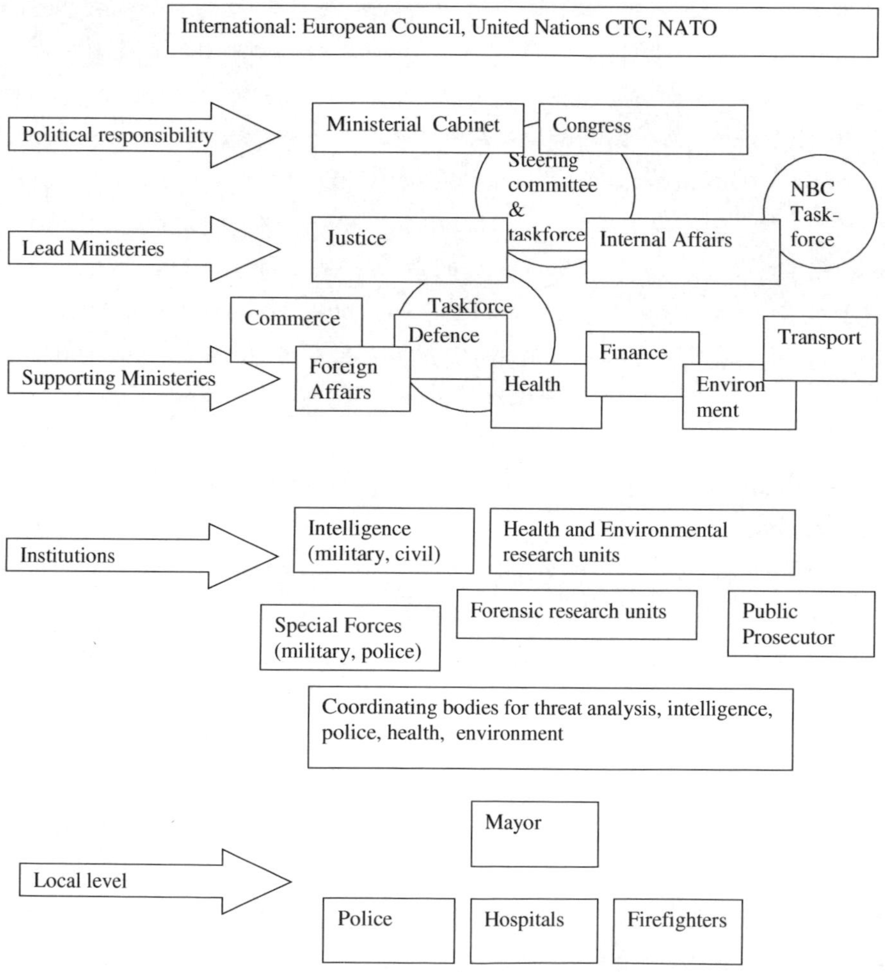

Fig 9. Organigram showing relations between political decision-making, governmental bodies and operational organisations relating to counter-terrorism in The Netherlands

Selected elements of national policymaking and implementation

The third and latest update to The Netherlands national action plan, named 'Combating International Terrorism' was sent to the House on 15 March 2002. It can be found in an abbreviated form in the Appendix. The action plan forms an integrated approach with the new version of the so-called 'National Handbook Crisis Decision making' that builds on existing policies, guidelines and experiences. The governments future focus is on the protection of critical infrastructures and vulnerabilities of the Dutch society, such as energy, water supply, food, telecommunication, transport, water management, finance, tax, public order and security, law enforcement, military, social security and various public objects such as bridges, tunnels, buildings, etc.

Prevention

The basis of the action plan concerns measures to prevent acts of terrorism. It concerns, first of all, preventive measures such as the improvement of the information position of police and intelligence and security services, liaison personnel, coordination centres, and more capacity for the protection and security of vulnerable persons (royalty, diplomatic corps, VIPs, dignitaries) and objects (total budget appropriated just over 8 million Euro). In order to deal effectively with the new types of terrorism, the intelligence and security services are provided with extra resources that amount to about 1.5 million Euro annually.

The security of Amsterdam International Airport Schiphol, the largest Dutch international airport, has been stepped up significantly, and will soon reach 100% capacity to scan all luggage. It already has reached full functionality to ensure proper clearance of all passengers and personnel. Operational security work is in large part carried out by private sector companies, but the Royal Military Constabulary is in control and carries the final responsibility. As Schiphol already was a very safe mainport, international independent reports have concluded that Schiphol now belongs to the best in the worldwide security class. Other, smaller airports and all domestic flight will eventually have to adhere to the same rules and regulations as Schiphol.

Visa and biometrics

Funds will also be made available to increase the opportunities for biometry. The use of physical characteristics is a valuable instrument in the identification of persons. It makes it easier to monitor terrorists and patrons and to unravel networks. From the point of view of prevention, The Netherlands wishes to stress, at a European level, the importance of an improved visa policy and centralizing the availability of information on visas issued within the Union, including biometric information. At this point, most of the focus is directed at improving content and accessibility of fingerprint databases. About 4.5 million Euro is allocated annually for fingerprint and visa R&D, databases and equipment. At a later stage, cutting edge biometry such as iris-scans and even DNA-profiling could come into play as well. For R&D in that field, a small amount of 0,2 million Euro is available. It is claimed that in general The Netherlands has taken a front row seat in biometrics and visa development and that other European countries are interested to learn more from the Dutch in this respect.

A second operational unit will be put in place to check the backgrounds of political refugees seeking asylum in The Netherlands ('1F' unit), with a budget of 1,36 million Euro mainly for personnel and training.

In addition, the Royal Netherlands Military Constabulary is expanded in order to intensify the external border controls and to strengthen the Mobile Border Supervision. There is a list of fourteen individual action points with respect to securing external borders and mobile surveillance, with a budget of over 1 million Euro. The measures taken after the attacks in the US to increase security of civil aviation are extended in line with the decisions of the Transport Council of the European Union of 14 September 2001, for example, by increased supervision and additional controls by the Royal Netherlands Military Constabulary. The Minister of Justice carries the final responsibility. Internationally (i.e. ICAO), The Netherlands argues for the introduction of 100% control of all hold baggage and improved security of the cockpit. Over 6 million Euro will be spent annually to increase airport security.

The government will also take measures to protect the infrastructure of the government and the corporate sector (including ICT), as well as critical infrastructures of society in general. The approach to this issue has just started with initial studies, and a workshop concerning the issue will follow. It is clear that the eventual effort will be major, integrative and multidisciplinary, and that a sizeable budget may be allocated. However, this focus of new counter-terrorism policy is yet in its infancy, and the final package for implementation will require several years of work.

Investigation and prosecution of terrorist crimes

The capacity for investigation and prosecution of terrorist crimes will be expanded considerably. Criminal investigators and analysts reinforce the Core teams, the Local and National Police Agencies[62] and the Public Prosecutions Department. The capacity of the human trafficking team at the Human Trafficking Unit is also expanded. In view of the fact that terrorist organisations often use modern technology, the government will also take measures in this field, such as creating a rapid reaction team at the national forensics laboratory, studies on cryptography and an action plan for digital investigation, the introduction of satellite interception capacity and the expeditious introduction of the National Action Plan on Digital Criminal Investigators and the modernization of police wiretapping rooms. The government has also decided to examine the capacity of the special assistance unit (BBE). In total an

[62] On 30 May 2002 it was decided by the newly installed Dutch Government that a Federal Bureau of Investigation will be realised, as opposed to the current situation of cooperating local bureaus.

annual budget of about 20 million Euro has been allocated. For technological measures a similar amount has been set-aside for the next two to three years.

Financial sector

The Ministry of Finance has issued lists of suspected individuals and institutions. This list was based in part on lists of the UN, the FBI, the White House, and later the EC. All Dutch banks and financial institutions cooperated to check the list with their administrative systems. Some assets were frozen immediately, blocking about 500.000 dollar in the first month after the attacks alone. It is fair to say however that after double checking, only the assets of the Bank of Afghanistan were blocked for a longer period, and at this point (April 2002) even those assets have been released again as the suspicion of terrorism-financing by the Bank of Afghanistan was lifted.

The relationship between capital flows and terrorist activity is of vital importance in the fight against terrorism. The government intends to put a halt to the supply of funds to terrorist groups in line with the Ecofin Council declaration of 21 September, emphasising the fight against money laundering. The measures with respect to the financial sector are divided into two groups. It concerns the financial supervision legislation and enforcement and the investigation of suspect flows of funds. The first group relates to a reinforcement of the supervision of the compliance with the Disclosure of Unusual Transactions Act (Wet MOT), the Identification Financial Services Act (Wet identificatie bij financiële dienstverlening) and the Sanctions Act (Sanctiewet) and a report obligation for independent (financial/legal) professionals and trust offices as well as regulations on supervision of trust offices and money transfer institutions. The second group of measures focuses on a reinforcement of the financial investigation, the improvement of the exchange of information and an efficient way of reporting information to the Unusual Transactions Reporting Office with respect to terrorism-related subjects.

Suspicious financial transactions will be identified by Dutch financial institutions under the aegis of the independent financial authority, working under the international umbrella of IOSCO.

International dimension

The fight against terrorism requires an international approach. International forums have taken initiatives in which The Netherlands participates. This includes, inter alia, the implementation of recommendations in the fight against money laundering by the Financial Task Force on Money Laundering (FATF), the obligation of States to make the provision of financial funds for terrorist activity punishable and a proposal by the European Council (21 September) that would enable, for example, The Netherlands to issue a court order to freeze assets in the event of serious suspicions against citizens of other EU Member States. The

Netherlands supports an active role of Europol in relevant information exchange at all possible levels. Also, it has strongly supported the development of a European arrest warrant. The Netherlands has also quickly provided its report to the CTC regarding Un resolution 1373.

With respect to operation enduring Freedom, The Netherlands has contributed with some F-16 reconnaissance aircraft. Also, a small number of Dutch Marines are engaged in peacekeeping and protection of parts of the infrastructure and personnel of the interim Afghan government.

Legislation

The Netherlands will stress the importance of rapid ratification of extradition treaties and the conclusion of the amended directive on money laundering. The Netherlands also participates in the implementation of the Framework Decrees on terrorism and the EU arrest warrant (end of 2001). At a national level, the legislation on UN Conventions on bomb terrorism and financing of terrorism must be ratified in timely fashion. Both legislative proposals have been submitted to the Lower House.

The Netherlands will undertake to ratify the EU agreement on mutual assistance. This would enable the formation of joint teams. In addition, the expeditious signing and ratification of the Convention on Crime in Cyberspace Convention is necessary.

There is national legislation underway to subdivide the country into 25 new 'security regions'. Within these regions, close collaboration between first responders is priority number one. All regions will have to develop multidisciplinary disaster reaction planning, based on local plans, which are in turn based on the local context, including vulnerabilities and capabilities.

First responders

It has become apparent that the information exchange between first responders (police, fire brigade, ambulance) needs professionalisation. Also some specific measures will have to be taken with respect to attacks with weapons of mass destruction, such as decontamination facilities that can be quickly set up at the site, as well as personal protection for the first responders themselves. Much of the response to nuclear, biological, chemical, radiological and informational attacks (NBCRI) can be dealt with using the existing structure of police, fire brigade, ambulance and the national structures supporting and coordinating them. For bio terrorism in particular a scenario handbook has been developed and the existing knowledge on diagnosis and prophylaxis has been surveyed, while additional R&D has been initiated to supplement that knowledge. New smallpox vaccine will be manufactured and stockpiled, as well as iodine prophylaxis for chemical attacks. The national coordination agency for infectious diseases (LCI) will provide protocols for diagnosis and treatment. A major training exercise with a smallpox pandemic outbreak is being planned as well as various environmental risk analyses. Also liaisons with research centres are institutionalised for rapid response when needed. Finally, the effects of NBCR attacks on food safety have been considered in participation with the food industry.

With regard to informational attacks (e.g. viruses, spams, denial of service, fraud, falsifying information etc) The Netherlands is committed to build on earlier initiatives taken in the realm of the Y2K strategy. An early warning centre is active.

Conclusions

Most of the post 9/11 response of the Dutch government to international terrorism has been - in line with its existing strategy – to try to prevent it. Therefore, the emphasis has been on increasing capabilities, capacity and coordination of intelligence. The effect of increased intelligence on security is potentially large, because daily updates of intelligence reports, through the technical evaluation centre, form an important input in the 'federal triangle', the institutionalised coordination of major national responsible authorities in The Netherlands, which, in turn, is continuously coordinated with the local triangles. The National coordination centre (NCC) is tasked with ensuring full coordination between national and local levels and between local levels. The Netherlands government believes that intelligence is the best-targeted instrument to receive early warning about upcoming threats or attacks – an instrument also that lends itself to targeted response measures. Targeted efforts are more efficient and effective than general efforts, such as foreign aid – an often falsely cited way of prevention. Although the Dutch government provides a large percentage of GDP (0,8 %; larger than any other country) to foreign aid and development, that effort (food and medicine, waterworks, education etc) is certainly not regarded as prevention of terrorism, because terrorism, in the view of the Dutch government, is not the result of poverty or 'failed states'. After all, in many past occasions, relatively wealthy individuals have initiated terrorism or have operated from wealthy countries, e.g., Osama Bin Laden, the Baader Meinhof Gruppe in Germany and, it seems, the anthrax attacker(s) in the USA. The same is true with respect to the issue of integration of political refugees. Refugees that do not integrate are not necessarily more prone to liaison with terrorist groups than others. Only those foreigners that deny the legal democratic law and order and do not integrate in any community – not the Dutch community, nor their own – are considered risky in the eyes of the AIVD. The Netherlands also has domestic policies to fight poverty and to improve inner cities. It even has a minister for inner city policy, who focuses on strengthening the relationships with foreign individuals and groups and the community. But terrorists may be left wing, centre, or right wing. They may be poor or they may be wealthy. They may operate in groups or solitarily. The boundary between terrorism and crime may be too small too make a distinction (after all, 'What is terrorism?' as the Minister of Justice recently said in the Congress security commission). There is just no way of discovering general patterns in advance that would support general preventative measures, the Dutch government believes. This is true for crime in general and terrorism in particular. Prevention of terrorism by targeted intelligence therefore clearly has the preference. However, the intelligence system cannot fully prevent attacks, unfortunately. Although many threats or planned attacks have been successfully dealt with in the past and recent past, some tragic events may still occur, as was shown as recently as may 6th 2002, when Mr. Fortuyn, a popular politician running for election in Congress, was assasinated. In the context of this study it may be characterized as an example of classical terrorism: threatening individuals with conventional weapons. Sofar, the Fortuyn as well as the Anthrax case indicate that terrorist attacks are committed by individuals who act on a strictly isolated basis, and are difficult to prevent from an intelligence point of view.

A general point that shapes Dutch counter-terrorism policy is that conventional weapons, including explosives, are being considered much more likely to be used in terrorism than unconventional weapons of mass destruction, such as nuclear, biological, radiological and even informational. Attacks with conventional weapons on NBC-related objects, transports or industries however are being considered to have disastrous effects. One spokesman called it 'Classical terrorism', indicating that the main focus of the Dutch government is on terrorists who use classical weapons on classical targets, such as a knife or a gun aimed at a specific person. As such, the 9/11 attacks were classical, because the terrorists used knives, one official said.

The Dutch government has shown a practical approach to post 9/11 counter-terrorism policymaking and implementation. First of all, the formation of steering committees and task forces provided focal points for the public in general, the media and the international community. Second, these groups set out to provide clear roadmaps and actions. These were made available to congress, but also to the public at large through the websites of various ministries. This created overall awareness. Practical emphasis was also put on the creation of budget to actually make the plans happen. This showed that the government is willing to 'put their money where their mouth is'. Not surprisingly, the reaction of the Congress security commission has been very favourable to the governments' response to international terrorism.

In addition, the discussion about the counter-terrorism regulatory and responsibility framework has clearly indicated that the government has good reason to believe that the current structure is capable of handling the threat of the new international terrorism to Dutch homeland as it is being perceived. And even although there is no centralized body that deals specifically with terrorism, it is clear that in most if not all cases, the Minister of Justice and The Minister of the Interior are in the lead, not withstanding the fact of course that is has been recognized that first responses to attacks and threats are local and that therefore the responsibility will be carried locally (by the Mayor).

As another aspect of The Netherlands' practical approach, we should mention that it is accepted that if terrorists are fanatically setting out to crate havoc, there will never be a 100% failsafe system that can combat it. Dutch society will never accept a 'Police State', and even slightly increasing the power of government to monitor individuals or groups in light of 9/11 or other terrorist attacks will encounter protests from various political and NGO groups that want to assure privacy.

The post 9/11 counter-terrorism policymaking and policy implementation in The Netherlands is running smoothly. The downside of that may be that it is running too smoothly. For, as a result, the public awareness is dropping, or at least it seems to be doing so. This seems mostly true for the general public and the media, but it may also be true for the awareness of some professional services. Critical structures such as water management installations, power generators and financial institutions for instance are no longer at an increased watch. The private sector has hardly taken its share yet (with some favourable exceptions, such as in the food industry). One sensitive item involving the private sector may be for instance Rotterdam Harbour where, as in harbours worldwide, security does not compare very well to airport security. While the Dutch government remains convinced of the raised likelihood of future threats and attacks, at the same it is not willing to issue warnings that are too general, because it is feared that general warnings in the long run will have an even more detrimental effect on awareness.

The best answer to this is perhaps training. The smallpox pandemic scenario is a good example, but if it is not covered in the media, it will not raise awareness at all relevant levels. Future training may therefore benefit from increased coverage by the media, as well by inclusion of all relevant bodies in the training exercise, not just including the Special Forces, but also the military in general.

The preliminary Netherlands matrix of challenges, measures, actors and stages, plus the status of progress is presented on the next pages. (Subcategories indicated in light gray follow from clustering by The Netherlands' authorities – not from the analytic framework)

Matrix of The Netherlands' challenges, measures, actors, stages and progress

CHS: Challenges as outlined
Msrs: Measures 1-Strategic, 2-Operational, 3-Tactical
Actors: 1-Public sector, federal/national level, civil (including special forces), 2-Public sector, 3-Regional/state level, civil, 4-Public sector, local level, civil, 5-Military, 6-Private sector
Sgs: Stages: 1-pre-attack, 2-trans-attack, 3-post-attack
Pgs: Progress: 1-No specific post 9/11 action; 2-Need for action identified, policy in the making; 3-Budget appropriated, actors identified; 4-Policy implementation well underway; 5-Policy implementation finalised

Nr	Description Netherlands post 9/11 policymaking and -implementation	Categorisation				Remarks (budgets in rounded figures kEuro per year)	Pgs
		Chs	Msrs	Ars	Sgs		
PREVENTION							
1	Continuous update of counter-terrorism policy and action plan	0	1	1	1-3	To the commission intelligence and safety of Congress	
2	Improved information exchange intelligence and police (NL, Europol)	0	2	1	1-3	National, bilateral, European and international	
	1. Rapid response of Task Force Police Chiefs to assignment of J&HA Council					Continuous (90)	3
	2. Expansion of interaction intelligence and security services					Realised (na)	5
	3. Rapid response of Europol to assignment of J&HA Council					Liaison of AIVD at Europol realised Liaison of KMAR upcoming (140)	5 4
	4. Foster international cooperation					Continuous (na)	1
	5. Expand national coordination centre public safety (LCOO) at joint national police services (KLPD)					Personnel and infrastructure realised 2002/2003 (590)	4
	6. Increase capacity of policy and coordination centre at Min. Interior					Realised (640)	5
VISA AND BIOMETRICS							
3	Biometrical identification	0	3	1	1-3	(fingerprint only as yet)	
	1. Centralized fingerprint database with rapid remote access						2
	2. Decentralized fingerprint equipment						2
	3. Coupling fingerprints and visa					(4,500 for research and procurement of equipment)	4
	4. R&D biometry and group monitoring					(230)	4
4	Harmonised visa policy	0	3	1	1	Negotiations in EU / R&D by EC	1
4a	Foundation of second operational '1F' unit	0	2	1	1	Personnel recruitment (1,360)	4
SURVEILLANCE, SECURITISATION AND PUBLIC ORDER							
5	Expansion capacity persons protection KLPD and KMAR	1	3	1	1		
	1. Expansion Royal and Diplomatic Protection Service (DKDB of KLPD)					KLPD is currently overstressed (1,405)	4
	2. Expansion Special Security Brigade and Special Safety Service (BSB BD/V of KMAR)					(2,500)	4
	3. Increase training capacity KMAR					(4,220)	4
6	Expansion of surveillance equipment	1	3	1	1		4
	1. Extra surveillance vehicles					Procurement process initiated (2002-2004: 15,000 total)	
	2. Extra fortified monitoring units						
	3. Renovation waterguns						
7	Securing external borders and mobile surveillance of aliens	0	3	1	1	14 individual action points focussing on borders and mainports: access to databases, personnel (hiring, training) and equipment for surveillance, monitoring and recognition. Budget partly allocated (> 1,000)	3
8	Additional measures for aviation safety	0	3	1	1	Goal: 100% check	
	1. Passengers and cabin baggage					(From levy on tickets)	5
	2. Luggage					(From levy on tickets)	5
	3. Personnel check					(From levy on tickets)	5

	4. Second inspection Justice					In line with EU transport council 7 December(180)	4
	5. Expansion KMAR					Hiring and training personnel (3,000)	4
	6. Securing telecom					Policy plan is ready (2,700)	3
9	Implementing the ECAC safety measures					Ongoing EU rules and regulations for civil aviation. ICAO: independent inspection of airports	3
10	Integrated package of measures to protect critical infrastructures	5,6	1	1	1-3	Major undertaking for many years to come	
	1. Quick Scan April 2002					A very important aspect, yet to be shaped. (Budget yet unknown but will be major)	4
	2. Workshop may 2002						3
	3. intermediate steps						2
	4. Final package (to be implemented)						1
IDENTIFICATION AND PROSECUTION OF TERRORIST CRIMES							
11	Expansion of capacity for research and analysis at various levels of criminal investigation	0	2	1	2-3	Justice, Police	
	1. Capacity at KLPD					(2,500) 42 fte	4
	2. Capacity at OM					(3,100)	4
	3. Capacity regional information desks					(3,400)	3
	4. Expansion regional information services					(910)	3
12	Quick Response team Forensics Research Institute (NFI-QRT) and expansion of NFI capacity	0	3	1	2-3		
	1. Building the NFI-QRT					(680) for 10 fte. Also a fully equipped mobile research station will have to be built (3117	4
	2. Increasing knowledge on biometry					(270)	3
	3. Digital research capability improvement					(340) plus (227) equipment	2
13	Expansion of the Unit Human Trafficking (UMS)	0	3	1	3		
	1. Increasing the capacity of UMS					(2,470)	3
	2. Improving the quality of information					(617)	2
	3. Border crossing research teams					(1,770)	2
	4. Inclusion of KMAR extra information					(599)	2
	5. Expansion public prosecution offices					(454)	2
TECHNOLOGICAL MEASURES							
14	Implementation of phone tapping requirements of the telecom law	0	2	1	1-3	Developing guidelines and enforcement rules	
	1. law implementation					(90)	
	2. law enforcement					(363)	
15	Speeding up the renovation of phone tapping equipment	0	3	1	1-3	Investment in new facilities for telephony and internet (12,600)	3
16	Initiatives and studies on Cryptography, Trusted Third Parties and access for police and intelligence						
	1. Self regulating of the telecom industry					Mostly taskforces etc. No special budget required	5
	2. Economic consequences study						5
	3. Legal basis for self regulation						3
	4. Evaluation of cryptography policy						2
17	Analysing the difficulties to intelligence by lack of harmonised regulation on length and kind of data storage by telecom providers	0	2	1	1-3	Research report (NA)	4
18	Expansion of satellite interception capability	0	3	1	1-3	Joint interception service of all intelligence and security services (2002-2005: 32,000)	3
19	Rapid realisation of national Action plan Digital Investigation (KLPD)	0	3	1	1-3	Hiring personnel, creating facilities (2001-2005: 1,5000)	3
INTEGRITY FINANCIAL SECTOR AND COMBATING TERRORISM TOTAL BUDGET (2,4000)							
20	Legal structure for the surveillance of money transfer offices	0	1	1	1	Result of FATF Washington October 2001 to avoid money laundering and financing of terrorism	4
21	Surveillance of trust offices	0	2	1	1	Connect with legal structure for financial services	3
22	Enforcing the law on reporting unusual financial transactions and related laws	0	2	1	1		
	1. law enforcement						4
	2. reporting duty						5
23	Increased strengthening of enforcement					Harmonising the approach,	3

	chain related to monitoring, identification, prosecution					improving information exchange, centralising prosecution and increasing capacity and knowledge.	
24	Strengthening the Financial Expertise Centre (FEC) for optimal information exchange					Joint centre	
	1. Check possibility participation of AIVD					(360)	3
25	Improving the capability for financial investigation in light of foreign request for help	0	3	1	1	(4,100)	3
26	Increasing information exchange with respect to 25	0	2	1	1		
27	Optimising the Reporting Centre for Unusual Transactions (MOT)	0	3	1	1	Very detailed improvement plan for financial-administrative and legal procedures within the boundaries of privacy requirements	4
28	Requirement for Fiscal and customs reporting on unusual transactions	0	2	1	1	Research activity	4
29	Reporting duty for entrepreneurs	0	2	3	1		
	1. expansion of current legal structure						5
	2. addition of insurance companies						3
30	na						
31	na						
32	Improve instruments to freeze suspicious accounts	0	3	1	1	Mostly legal instruments TBD	3
33	na						
RESPONDING TO TERRORISM							
34	Analysis and expansion of special forces capacity at Police and Marines	0	3	1,4	2,3	(8,660) 65 fte	4
35	Extra support by defence	0	2	4	2,3	(4,500) report ready	2
OTHER LEGAL ASPECTS							
36	Rapid ratification of international treaty on extradition	0	1	1	3	(na)	2
37	Rapid legal framework against money laundering and for reporting duty for unusual transactions in the private sector	0	1	1	1	(na)	2
38	European terrorism and arrest warrant legal framework	0	1	1	1,3	(na)	4
39	Ratify and implement UN resolutions on bomb terrorism and financing of terrorism	0	1	1	1,3	(na)	4
40	Ratify EU legal assistance agreement	0	1	1	1-3	Includes the possibility of creating joint teams (na)	3
41	Sign and implement the EU resolution on Crime in Cyberspace	6	1	1	1-3	(na)	4
42	Protocol for compulsory information provision by financial institutions	0	2	1	1,3	(na)	3
43	Research legal obstacles to international information sharing in criminal investigations	0	2	1	1,3	(na)	4
TERRORISM AND NBC							
44	Prepare for bio terrorism	4,6	3	1	2,3		
	1. Bioterrorism scenario handbook						5
	2. Survey knowledge and experience on micro-organism diagnostics (RIVM)						5
	3. RIVM project on diagnostics						5
	4. Produce extra smallpox vaccine						4
	5. National Coordination Entity (LCI) will expand and produce new treatment protocols						5
	6. prepare large scale drill smallpox-pan demy						4
	7. Implement EU Health Council conclusions						5
45a	Other NBC preparation	4,6	3	1	2,3		
	1. NBC report to congress						5
	2. Environmental risk analysis						5
	3. Stockpiling Iodium prophylaxis						4
	4. EU action plan for disaster response and management coordination					ongoing	3
45b	Follow up of environmental risk analysis	4,6	3	1	1,3	(1,300)	
	1. Increase knowledge and experience tap water safety						5
	2. Strengthen capacity of Policy Support						4

	team for environmental disasters (BOT-mi)						
	3. Install BOT-mi						5
	4. Contracts with knowledge centres on chemical warfare agents (TNO)						5
	5. Create central environment response team with protective gear						5
	6. Increase capabilities and capacity national information centre						4
	7. Strengthen the environmental research service						4
	8. Research critical concentrations of chemicals						4
46	Safeguarding food safety under NBC terrorist attack	4,6	2	1	1		
	1. Quick scan food safety risks						5
	2. Information exchange with industry branch organisations						5

Spain

General overview

Background

Spain has lived under the threat of terrorism for several decades. The terrorist group ETA (Euskadi ta Askatasuna) has killed over 800 people since 1968 (Figure 10).

Figure 10. July 1997, San Sebastian. At least 20,000 people took to the streets in this northern city, shouting slogans in support of Basque independence and the militant separatist organization ETA

Fighting for an independent Basque country in the northeastern Spain and southwestern France, ETA also engages in kidnapping, extortion, threats, and vandalism. As such, Spanish authorities at all levels deal with terrorism on a 'daily' basis. To counter these threats, Spain has a well-developed counter terrorist infrastructure spanning from elite autonomous police forces to specialized powerful judges with far reaching competencies[63].

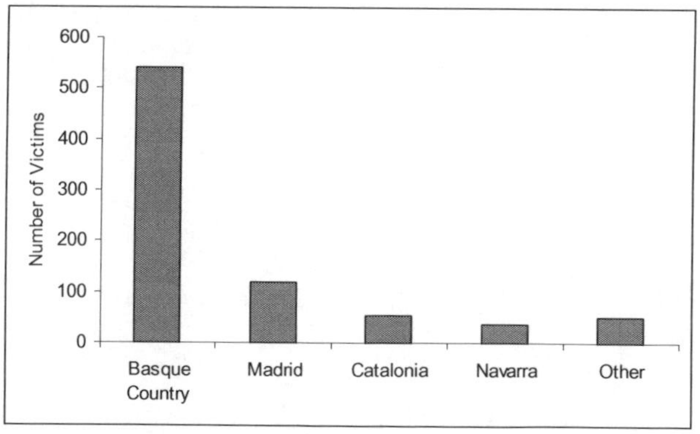

Figure 10- Number of ETA Victims: By Autonomous Region

[63] Judge Baltasar Garzón—a member of the Audiencia Nacional (National High court) was the first justice official outside the US to round up and accuse Islamic suspects in the 9/11 attacks.

Reactions to 9/11

Immediately after the 11 September[th] attacks, the Spanish government activated a crisis cell (célula de crisis)[64]. Members of the cell include President Aznar, Interior Minister Rajoy, Defence Minister Trillo, Foreign Affairs Minister Piqué, government spokesman Cabanilla, Secretary General of the Presidency Zarzalejos, Secretary of State for Security Morenés, and the Director of the International Defence Department (Gil-Casares).

The cell's primary purpose is to coordinate the adoption of ensuing security measures; specifically, the directives established by the First Deputy Prime Minister and the Minister of the Interior[65]. The Director General of the Infrastructure and Crisis Response Department (DISC) maintains communications and coordinates information during the existence of the cell. Examples of measures implemented after the attacks include enhanced airport security, increased airspace surveillance, increased border security, and placing all police dependencies under maximum alert. Security has also been increased at the military bases of Rota and Morón—where American personnel are typically present—and at the US and Israeli embassies. It should be noted that Spain is dedicating assets and personnel to Operation Enduring Freedom in Afghanistan.

As the holder of the EU Presidency, Spain has forcefully come out against terrorism. Its aim is to prioritise the fight against terrorism by pushing for greater cooperation and coordination at the European level. Hoping to maintain the spotlight on terrorism, some of Spain's priorities currently include:

- Converging all the legal systems of the Union's Member States to eradicate any possibility of terrorist sanctuary in the territory of the EU;
- Strengthening the necessary legislative and judicial instruments, specifically the framework Decision on the Combating of terrorism, the framework Decision on the European arrest warrant, the framework decision on the freezing of assets, the mutual recognition of judgments, and support for Eurojust (formalized in 2002);
- Continuing work on the common lists of terrorist organizations, joint investigation teams, and the strengthening of Europol;
- Steeping up cooperation in criminal matters; encouragement for the creation of a European network to train magistrates; and
- Launching a debate for the inclusion of fighting terrorism as an ESDP objective.

Since 9/11, Spain has strengthened its dialogue with the United States, with the Bush administration at the governmental level and the FBI at the operative level.

---

[64] This is not a new cell; for example, it has been activated previously during natural disasters and during the Kosovo war.

[65] Declaration by President Aznar in Tallin (Estonia) on 11 September[th], 2001.

Some characteristics of the national institutional framework[66]

The following organigram provides an overview of the main Spanish organizations involved in anti-terrorist work.

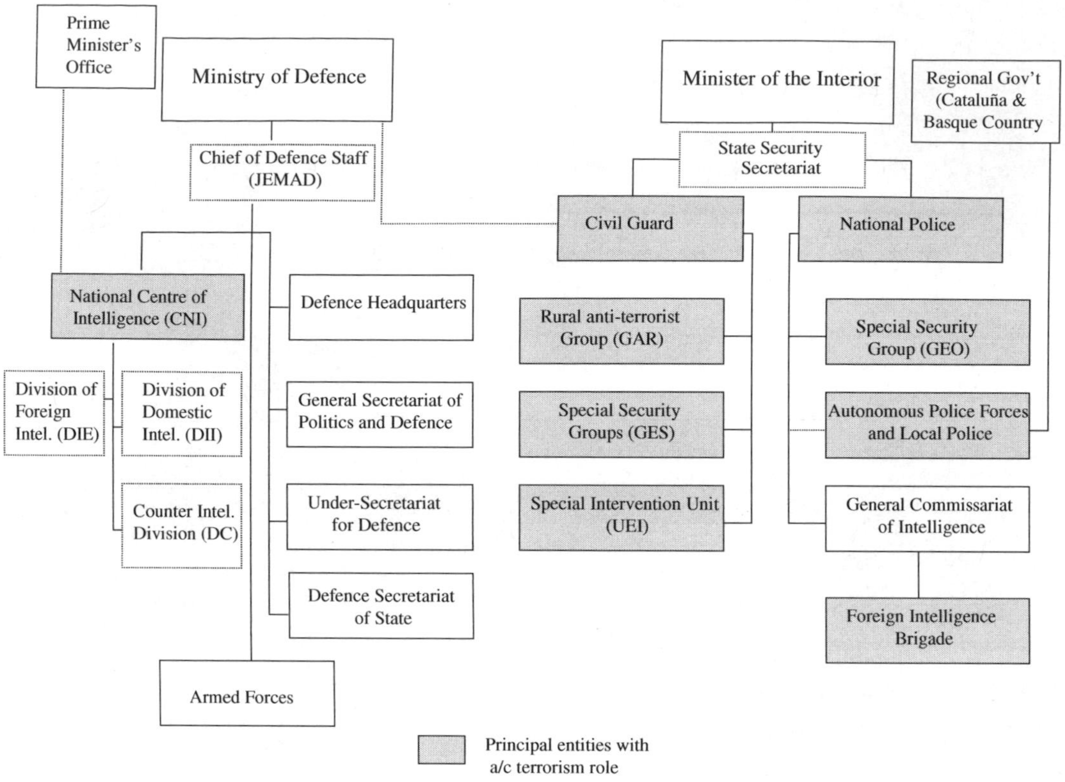

Figure 12- Organigram of Relevant Spanish Agencies Concerned with Anti-Terrorism

Ministry of Defence

The principal agency tasked with fighting terrorism under the Ministry of Defence is the former Higher Defence Intelligence Centre (CESID)—currently known as the National Centre of Intelligence (CNI). Controlled by the Prime Minister's office, it focuses on both foreign and domestic intelligence; its domestic portfolio is geared towards counter-terrorist intelligence.

Ministry of the Interior

Under the Ministry of the Interior are the Guardia Civil and the National Police. The Civil Guard finds its roots from the French Gendarmerie. Headed by a civilian director general since 1986, it is accountable to the Interior Ministry via the State Security Secretariat. The

[66] Sources: Federation of American Scientists, Jane's Information Group, Spanish Ministry of Defence, Spanish Ministry of the Interior, and the Official Bulletin of the State (BOE).

Civil Guard polices rural areas and controls borders and highways[67]. It is also responsible for firearms and explosive control, ports, airports, border patrol, and border control. In addition, the Civil Guard counts with more specialized units (GAR, GES, UEI), including special anti-terrorist units posted in the Basque, neighbouring Navarra, and along the French border. It should be noted that the Defence Ministry remains partially responsible for the Civil Guard during wartimes. The Ministry of Defence and Ministry of Interior have joint responsibility in areas of recruitment, and weapons, and training.

Headed by a Director General under the auspices of the Interior Ministry, the National Police handle national investigations, security in urban areas, traffic control, and hostage rescue. It tends to be concentrated in urban areas and has both uniformed and plain-clothed officers. The centrally controlled Special Security Group (GEO) is an elite-fighting unit trained to deal with terrorist and hostage situations. The Ertzaintza and Mossos d'Escuadra (not listed in the organigram) are autonomous police forces under the regional governments of the Basque Country and Cataluña respectively.

The National Police Corps also includes the General Commissariat of Intelligence that has an antiterrorist mission. Its Foreign Intelligence Brigade is used to investigate international terrorism aimed against Spain. (FAS).

Selected elements of national policymaking and implementation

Spain's counter terrorist policies post 9/11 have been principally geared at maintaining or augmenting current counter-terrorism efforts. This has been achieved by stimulating intelligence sharing and formulating contingency plans in the event of an attack. For example, Spain has a specific plan of action to be implemented in the event of a terrorist attack with conventional weapons. Measures have also taken to encourage greater coordination between agencies involved in counter terror coupled with the establishment of new entities to cover 'new' terrorist areas.

In summary, measures adopted at the domestic level include:[68]

- Preventative and rapid-response measures to neutralise a terrorist attack or attempted attack with chemical or biological materials;
- Intensified control over goods that could be used to manufacture weapons of mass destruction;

[67] In the Basque Country, the autonomous police forces have taken over many of the duties of the Civil Guard.

[68] United Nations Security Council (S/2001/1246), "Letter dated 21 December 2001 from the Chairman of the Security Council Committee established pursuant to resolution 1373 (2001) concerning counter-terrorism addressed to the President of the Security Council.

- An operational preventative plan for studying and gaining knowledge about the ideology, objectives, modus operandi of terrorist organizations; and
- Intensified efforts to trace the possible contacts of persons in Spain with organisations of concern.

Bio-Chemical Emergency Plan

Post 9/11, the Ministry of Defence activated a pre-established operational preventative rapid-response plan to neutralise a chemical or biological attack. Over 250 soldiers assigned to the nuclear, chemical, and biological units (NBQ) between Valencia, Burgos, and Madrid are on high alert[69]. The units have established a priority list to prevent possible attacks. A certain number of public hospital beds have been reserved should there be a contingency while a permanent line of communication has been established between the Ministry of Defence and the Ministry Health. Since the US anthrax attacks, Spain—resembling the experience of many other countries—has had over 2,000 'false alarms' with questionable packets.

Civilian authorities are paying closer attention to purchases of certain materiel—for example, the acquisition of machinery for the elaboration of chemical components or fertilizer. Spain does not foresee a higher threat picture warranting additional measures. Not surprisingly, according to the spokesperson for the Directorate General of Civilian Protection (DGPC), local civilian agencies do not have a contingency plan in case of an attack[70]. Similarly, the head of the fire department headquarters in Madrid notes that they do not have a specific plan in the event of a bio-chemical attack. There level of preparation is marginal at best[71].

At the European level, Spain has forwarded the idea of a EU study to investigate European NBC capabilities and its associated early warning resources.

Preventive Measures

The 11 September[th] attacks breathed new life into Spain's Higher Defence Intelligence Centre (CESID); renamed the National Centre of Intelligence (CNI) on October 2001. Presently, there is a draft proposal on the table to expand the powers of the CNI[72]. For example, the proposal suggests that in future urgent cases related to terrorism, CNI officials would have the right to intercept communications and enter residences without the prior permission of a judge. The judge would be notified *a posteriori* for ratification or non-authorization[73]. The

---

[69] Similarly, NBQ units under the Special Intervention Unit (Guardia Civil) have been prepared to handle events such as industrial spillages of hazardous materials.

[70] DGPC is responsible for coordinating all civilian assets in case of an attack.

[71] "Defensa activa un Plan de Emergencia ante Posibles Atentados Químicos y Biológicos", *El Mundo*, October 14, 2001.

[72] President Aznar gave his nod of approval to the draft on October 9th 2001. The draft has to go through the General Council of Judicial Power, the State Council, and Parliament for final approval.

[73] "Consenso en Torno al Proyecto del CNI", Revista Española de Defensa, Numero 165, November 2001 and "España: Los Agentes del Cesid podrán entrar en las casas sin permiso judicial previo", *El País*, October 10, 2001.

momentum behind this push is to give the CNI more teeth to pre-emptively strike at future terrorist attacks.

A related and long-standing project is the creation of delegated commission, a community of intelligence to ensure coordination between the CNI and other information gathering organizations—especially those linked to the Guardia Civil and National Police. The commission is to be headed by First Deputy Prime Minister Rajoy and would count with the participation of the ministers of defence, interior, state, the director of CNI (with the rank of state secretary), and the state secretaries for state security and the presidency[74].

Potential Future Developments

The Interior Ministry has prepared a draft project to create a new Commission for Monitoring Terrorism Financing Activities (Comisión de Vigilancia de Actividades de Financiación del Terrorismo). It is envisioned that this Commission will be able to investigate and block—without previous judicial authorization—all banking transactions in which people or entities associated with terrorism are involved. The Commission will be able to freeze questionable assets up to six months, with additional blockage requiring authorization by a judge.

The establishment of the Commission would forge greater cooperation between the social security administration, the central bank, the National Administration for Insurance and Pensions, and other organizations with a supervisory role in financial matters. The make-up of the Commission will consist mostly of government representatives from the Ministries of Finance, Justice, Interior, and Defence. Previously, only judges could take preventive measures to block accounts *a posteriori* if they thought they had served to finance terrorism. The constitutionality dimensions of the proposal are still being debated[75].

Financial Dimension

Up to this point (May 2002), no additional financial packages have been passed to cover the increased security expenditures incurred since 9/11. Thus, it is the 2002 budget (and increasingly the 2003 budget) that has been absorbing the costs. Spain's largest expenditure stems from its military contribution to Operation Enduring Freedom in Afghanistan. The costs associated with the maintenance of some 350 personnel and other attached elements (including ships) may force the government to announce a 'supplement extraordinaire' later this year[76]. It should be noted that the government's 2002 budget froze the amount of reserved funds—those not requiring parliamentary or ministerial accountability—held by the Interior, Exterior and Defence Ministries, for the second year in a row.

---

[74] "El Gobierno vincula la reforma del Cesid a la nueva situación creada tras el 11 de septiembre", *El Mundo*, October 13, 2001.

[75] "La Ley para bloquear fondos terroristas plantea 'serias dudas de constitucionalidad'", *El Mundo*, February 3rd 2002.

[76] It is foreseen that the troops will operate in Afghanistan until the end of June.

Conclusions

ETA has been and continues to be the principal threat on Spanish soil—even though there is increased awareness of the global nature and reach of terrorism. As recently as February 2002, Basque Interior Minister Javier Balza launched an in-depth reform of the anti-terrorist intelligence services administered by the Ertzaintza (autonomous Basque police) to fortify the efforts against ETA[77]. Fears of an impending ETA attack were visible in the significant security precautions implemented during the EU Summit held in Barcelona in mid-March 2002. Force deployments to prevent an attack included thousands of riot police, F-18 fighter aircraft, NATO AWACS patrolling the skies, and warships around the port area. Efforts such as these simultaneously serve to identify and dismantle other terrorist elements. For example, a police raid (Operation Dátil) on November 13th 2001, led to the arrest of thirteen individuals linked to Al Qaeda / Osama Bin Laden.[78] On April 24th, 2002, Spanish police arrested Syrian-born Mohammed Galeb Kalaje Zouaydi on suspicions of playing a support role for the 11 Septemberth attacks.

Spain's reactions to the 9/11 attacks can be characterized as a bolstering of internal security while using the political arena to call for stronger anti/counter terrorist legislation. The relative simplicity of these reactions can be traced to two principal factors.

First, Spain has traditionally had a strong and well-functioning domestic counter terrorist apparatus. For example, in the Basque region, four separate security forces—local police, regional police, national police and the Guardia Civil—are responsible for security. With 8,000 national security personnel and 7,000 Ertzaintza operating in the region, the ratio of security force personnel to citizens is approximately 1:135[79]. As such, the events of 9/11 have served to reinforce and maintain an already sophisticated anti-terrorist system. Improvements have been targeted at increasing organizational coordination while boosting intelligence.

Second, as the current holder of the EU Presidency, Spain has seized the opportunity to posit the need to combat terrorism at the European level. The objective is to deny would-be terrorists sanctuary in any of the fifteen EU Member States. According to Spanish authorities, an important step in this direction would be to coordinate and synergise current European anti-terrorist policies. According to First Deputy Prime Minister Rajoy, "combating terrorism will be the Spanish Presidency's priority"[80].

---

[77] Jane's Information Group 2002.
[78] Earlier, a six man cell with ties to Islamic terrorists was dismantled on September 26th 2001.
[79] Jane's Information Group 2002.
[80] Spanish EU Presidency, February 2nd 2002.

Matrix of Spain's challenges, measures, actors, stages and progress

CHS: Challenges as outlined
Msrs: Measures 1-Strategic, 2-Operational, 3-Tactical
Actors: 1-Public sector, federal/national level, civil (including special forces), 2-Public sector, 3-Regional/state level, civil, 4-Public sector, local level, civil, 5-Military, 6-Private sector
Sgs: Stages: 1-pre-attack, 2-trans-attack, 3-post-attack
Pgs: Progress: 1-No specific post 9/11 action; 2-Need for action identified, policy in the making; 3-Budget appropriated, actors identified; 4-Policy implementation well underway; 5-Policy implementation finalised

Nr	Description Spain post 9/11 policymaking and -implementation	Categorisation				Remarks	Pgs
		Chs	Msrs	Ars	Sgs		
PREVENTION							
1	Greater information sharing between organizations involved in counter-terrorism	0	1	1	1-3		
	1. Greater cooperation between Ministry of Defence and Interior Ministry						1
	2. Foster international cooperation					European Level and with US (especially FBI)	1
INFRASTRUCTURE PROTECTION							
2	Pre-established protection of critical /sensitive infrastructures	0	3	1	1-3		
	1. Security enhancements at military bases					Rota and Moron (known for US presence)	5
SURVEILLANCE, SECURITISATION AND PUBLIC ORDER							
3	Additional measures for aviation safety	0	3	1	1		5
4	Securing internal borders and airspace	0	3	1,2,4	1-3		
	1. Increased airspace surveillance						5
	2. Reform of Ertzaintza					Basque territory	2
	3. Increased protection around US and Israeli embassies						4
	4. Increased security along public areas						4
	5. Expansion in number of law enforcement assets devoted to protection					Total force goal for National Police in general: 52,000 personnel; goal for Guardia Civil 73,000	2
	6. Law enforcement on maximum alert						
5	Increased surveillance	0	1	1	1-3		
	1. Intensified efforts to trace possible contacts of persons with organizations of concern						2
TERRORISM AND NBC							
6	Protection against NBC threats	4,6	3	1,4	2-3		
	1. Activation of pre-established plan						5
	2. NBC soldiers on alert						
	3. Alert of NBC units under Guardia Civil						
	4. Priority list to prevent attacks						5
	5. Greater surveillance of hazardous material purchases (e.g. fertilizer)						4
	6. Designation of certain number of hospital beds for biological emergencies						5
	7. Permanent line of communication between Ministry of Defence and Ministry of Health						5
	8. Intensified control over goods that could be used to manufacture wmd						4
INTEGRITY FINANCIAL SECTOR AND COMBATING TERRORISM							
7	Greater Financial Surveillance	0	1,2	1	1		
	1. Potential creation of Commission for Monitoring Terrorism Financing Activities						2
	2. Greater cooperation envisioned between social security administration, central bank, and others						2
	3. Improved instruments to freeze suspicious accounts and transactions						2
NATIONAL INTELLIGENCE							
8	Revamping of CESID	0	1,2	1	1		

	1. CESID 're-invented' as CNI						4
	2. More room for preemptive searches						2
	3. Establishment of a community of intelligence for greater coordination					Delegated Commission headed by First Prime Minister	2
TECHNOLOGICAL MEASURES							
9	Expansion in use of technological aides	0	2	1	1		
	1. Greater rights to intercept communications					CNI	
EUROPEAN UNION							
10	Measures at European Union level	0	1, 2	1	1		
	1. Greater cooperation in matters relating to terrorism						1
	2. Terrorism as priority on EU agenda during Spanish EU Presidency						1
	3. Proposal for EU study on EU NBC capabilities and early warning						1
	4. Strengthen legal systems to deny terrorist sanctuary in EU						1
	5. Increased cooperation in criminal matters						2
	6. Continued work on common list of terrorist organizations						4
	7. Continued work on establishment of joint investigation teams						2
	8. European terrorism and arrest warrant legal framework						4
	9. Strengthening Europol						
	10. Terrorism as an ESDP objective (debate)						1
OTHER							
11	International military operations	0	1	1,4	1,3		
	1. Participation in Operation Enduring Freedom						4

United Kingdom

General overview

Background

Terrorism is not new to the United Kingdom, either domestically or internationally. In modern times, The UK has dealt with terrorist activities throughout its colonies during the 1950-1970 periods of decolonisation – usually implementing a policing-based counter-insurgency strategy to confront these – as well as through the ongoing threat of modern Irish terrorist activities (directed against British interests – at any given time – from both the Loyalist/Unionist/Protestant and Republican/Nationalist/Catholic sides) since the late-1960s. Further to this, British personnel – long actively high profile throughout Europe and elsewhere – have faced the threat of terrorism against both their representatives and citizens abroad.

More recently, The UK has been faced – even before the attacks of 11 September 2001 – with growing concerns over terrorist acts perpetrated domestically by émigré groups existent within The UK. While this has stemmed – and been most public – largely from and around the Islamic and Sikh/Asian communities, other ethno-nationalist groups (such as those from the Balkans or the Middle East) have been faced with similar violence within The UK. Indeed, British authorities have long had to deal with the threats presented by third-party foreign activities being perpetrated within The UK against individuals (such as exile communities) resident in The UK, but not necessarily THE UK nationals. Consequently, the law enforcement powers and legislation which have developed in The UK to confront terrorism had long examined any number of possible incidents for terrorist activities – as well as always ensuring (the primary trend) that terrorist acts would be responded to first and foremost as illegal (i.e. criminal) activities, with law enforcement being primary.

Fig. 13 Mahem after 2001 IRA attack in Omagh, Ireland

Reactions to 9/11[81]

In summary, since 11 September 2001, Britain has taken the following steps to combat Al Qaeda and the wider terrorist threat:

[81] Extracted primarily from *Report to the Counter-Terrorism Committee pursuant to paragraph 6 of Security Council Resolution 1373(2001) of 28 September 2001* (20 December 2001).

- Development of a broad international coalition against terrorism, in which a wide range of countries, including Arab and Muslim states, have played a part, from the granting of landing and overflight rights to the sharing of intelligence;
- Successful military action against Al Qaeda and the Taliban regime;
- Support for the establishment of an Interim Administration in Afghanistan committed to combating terrorism;
- Deployment of British troops as part of a UN-authorised International Security Assistance Force to promote stability in Afghanistan;
- Preventive measures against terrorist attacks on The UK;
- Introduction of the Anti-Terror Act and detention of foreign nationals suspected of involvement in terrorism;
- Implementation of UN Resolution 1373 on counter-terrorism measures;
- Agreement of an EU Action Plan against terrorism including enhanced police and judicial co-operation and strengthened air security; and
- Increased international assistance to states that oppose terrorist activity.

The UK outlined its objectives in the domestic and global fights against terrorism in a 16 October speech to the House of Commons by Foreign Secretary Jack Straw. Stating that "Our overall objective is to eliminate terrorism as a force in international affairs", he outlined the immediate objectives as:

- To bring Osama Bin Laden and other Al Qaeda leaders to justice;
- To prevent Osama Bin Laden and the Al Qaeda network from posing a continuing terrorist threat;
- To this end to ensure that Afghanistan ceases to harbour and sustain international terrorism and enables us to verify that terrorist training has ceased and that the camps where terrorists train have been destroyed; and
- Assuming that Mullah Omar will not comply with the US ultimatum we require sufficient change in the leadership to ensure that Afghanistan's links to international terrorism are broken.

The wider objectives of the war are:

- To do everything possible to eliminate the threat posed by international terrorism;
- To deter states from supporting, harbouring or acting complicity with international terrorist groups;
- Reintegration of Afghanistan as a responsible member of the international community and an end to its self-imposed isolation.

The immediate objectives were to be achieved by all available means, including both political and military:

- Isolating the current Taliban regime from all international support.

- Unless the Taliban regime complies with the US ultimatum, taking direct action against Osama Bin Laden, the Al Qaeda networks and the terrorist facilities in Afghanistan, and where necessary taking political and military action to fragment the present Taliban regime, including through support for Pashtun groups opposed to the regime as well as forces in the Northern Alliance.
- Providing economic and political support to Afghanistan's neighbours to help with the burden of this conflict.
- Building the widest possible international coalition, with maximum UN support.
- Taking immediate steps to deal with the humanitarian crisis confronting Afghanistan and to help neighbouring countries deal with the refugee problem.

The wider campaign will be conducted on a broad front:

- To make a step change in international efforts to change the climate in which terrorists operate. This will be a complex campaign including strengthening domestic legislation and national capabilities and working through the United Nations, European Union and G8 to cut off the terrorists' funds and make it easier to trace terrorists and bring them to justice
- Reconstruction of Afghanistan. Realistically it will be difficult for this to start until there is a secure environment within Afghanistan. But a programme of emergency relief will have to be available early. The cost of reconstructing Bosnia was $5bn and Afghanistan has four times Bosnia's population. Reconstruction of Afghanistan could take 5-10 years to complete. Only sustained international development effort has any chance of ridding Afghanistan of heroin and domination of warlords
- Assisting Afghanistan, including through the United Nations, to establish a broadly based government representative of all groups in the country
- A positive political agenda of engagement with Arab countries and the Islamic world
- A strategy to deal with the wide number of sometimes-small groups of terrorists who flourish in states across the world and the linkages between them. This will include sustained pressure on those states that aid and abet terrorism. Where states are powerless to put a stop to terrorism on their territory assistance will have to be made available. Where states are unwilling to take effective action they will face a vigorous response from the wider international community
- Renewed efforts to resolve the conflicts which are among the underlying causes of terrorism; and renewed efforts to bear down on Weapons of Mass Destruction proliferation

Some characteristics of the national institutional framework

The Home Secretary stated in October 2001 that at the time of the Millennium a great deal of work was undertaken to ensure the security of key utilities. He assures the House that both in the Civil Contingencies Committee and more widely, the government had examined and put in place, further work to update our preparedness, preventive action, and remedial steps, should they be necessary.

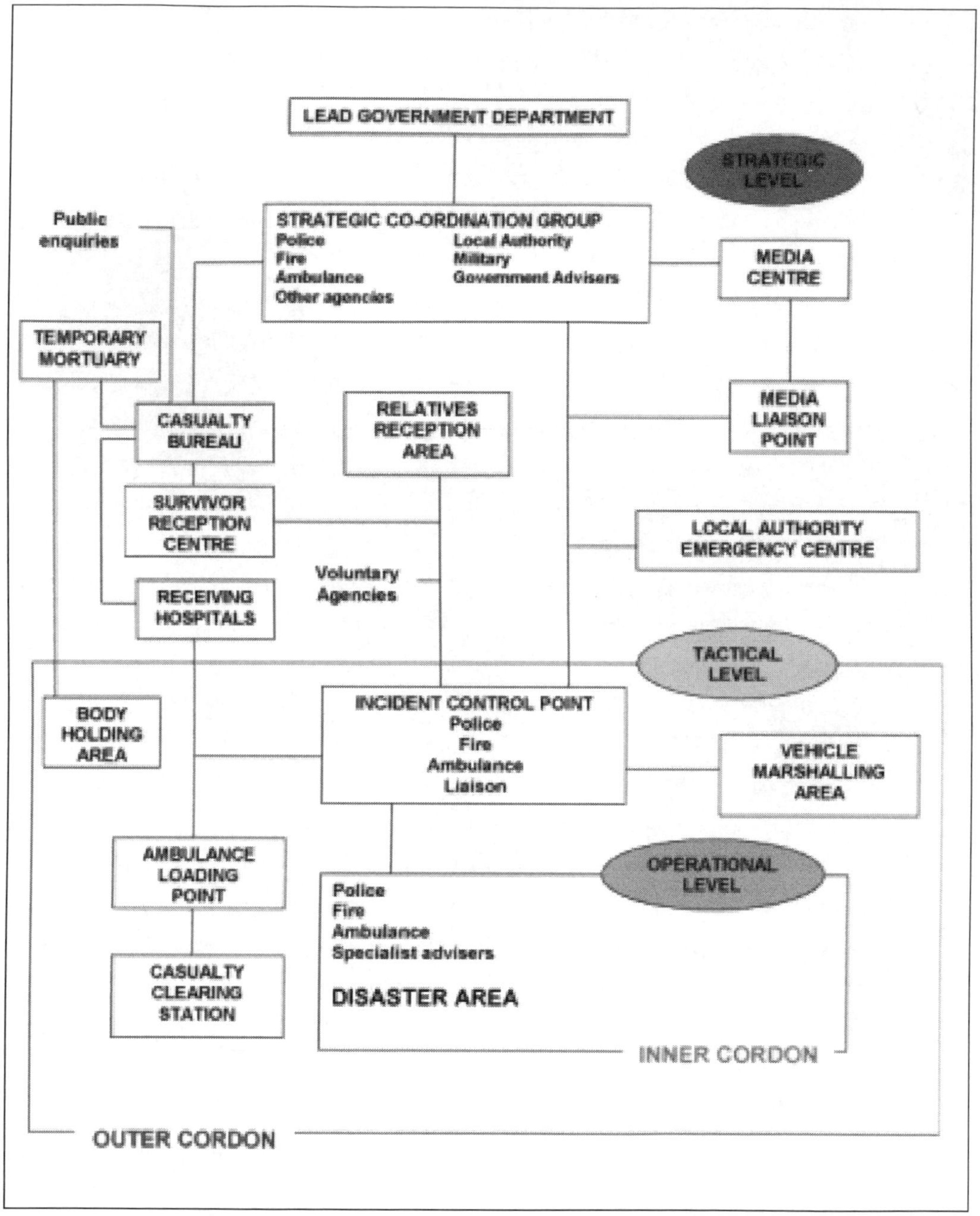

Fig 14. Organigram of Responsive Authorities for Disaster (including Terrorism) Management

State Structures Responsible for Terrorism

Central Government

Overall in The UK, primary responsibility for confronting terrorism rests with the Cabinet Office and the machinery of central government. From here, the rest of the government (for example, the Home Office who has a number of lead-agencies concerned with terrorism, or the Ministry of Defence, which confronts terrorism both internally – vis-à-vis Northern Ireland – or internationally) is directed. In terms of immediate co-ordination of responses, while longer-term co-ordination occurs through these Cabinet Office Secretariats, initial co-ordination almost invariably begins through the government emergency co-ordinating committee known as COBRA (for 'Cabinet Office Briefing Room A' where it meets). COBRA is comprised currently of the Deputy Prime Minister; the Cabinet Secretary, the Foreign Secretary, the Chancellor, the Defence Secretary, the Home Secretary, the Chief of Defence Staff, the Chairman of the Joint Intelligence Committee, and the Chief Foreign Policy Adviser to the Prime Minister – and, on an ad hoc basis, the Director-General of the Security Service, the Director General of the Secret Intelligence Service, the Director of Communications & Strategy in the PMO, the Director of Government Relations in the PMO, the Chief of Staff in the PMO. COBRA has met on average once a week since the military action in Afghanistan began.

Alongside COBRA are the individual Cabinet Committees. Under the Cabinet Committee System, The UK has the following primary Cabinet Committees involved in the War on Terrorism (CCC and DOP (IT) primary).

Ministerial Civil Contingencies Committee (CCC): includes the Secretary of State for the Home Office (Chair) and others – including Number 10, the Cabinet Office, Treasury and the devolved administrations – will be invited to attend, depending on the contingency. It "co-ordinates the preparation of plans for ensuring in an emergency the supplies and services essential to the life of the community; to keep these plans under regular review; and to supervise their prompt and effective implementation in specific emergencies." The Committee has been particularly active since 11 September. Three committees, chaired by Ministers, support the work of the CCC. They are The UK Resilience Committee (chaired by Chris Leslie, Cabinet Office); the London Resilience Committee (chaired by Nick Raynsford, Minister for London); and the CBRN Committee – preparedness for a chemical, biological, radiological or nuclear incident (chaired by John Denham, Home Office).

The Cabinet Office Civil Contingencies Secretariat (see below) has been very busy supporting those committees, by:

- Making sure all contingency plans are reviewed and renewed in the light of new threats
- Making sure all reasonable precautions are taken
- Making sure guidance is brought up to date

- Making sure government has good communication systems in place
- Making sure The UK is as well-prepared as possible
- Making sure everyone knows how they fit into the overall picture – whether they work in the emergency services or in central, local or devolved government

The CCC also ensures that a Lead Government Department (LGD) is nominated in good time to respond to an emergency rests with the Cabinet Office, as part of its normal role in co-ordinating activities which involve a number of government departments. It is also responsible for ensuring that the LGD arrangements are properly implemented when an emergency occurs.

Ministerial Sub-Committee on International Terrorism (DOP (IT)): includes the Prime Minister (Chair), the Deputy Prime Minister and First Secretary of State, the Chancellor of the Exchequer, the President of the Council and Leader of the House of Commons, the Secretary of State for Foreign and Commonwealth Affairs, the Secretary of State for the Home Department, the Secretary of State for International Development, and the Secretary of State for Defence. In addition, the Chief of the Defence Staff and the Attorney General will attend as required. Other Ministers and Heads of the Intelligence Agencies will also be invited to attend as necessary. It "keeps under review the Government's policy on international terrorism, in particular the political, military and humanitarian response to the attacks in the United States on 11 September and preventive security measures in the United Kingdom and overseas."

Ministerial Committee on Defence and Overseas Policy (DOP): includes the Prime Minister (Chair), the Deputy Prime Minister and First Secretary of State, the Chancellor of the Exchequer, the Secretary of State for Foreign and Commonwealth Affairs, the Secretary of State for International Development, the Secretary of State for Defence, and the Secretary of State for Trade and Industry. It "keeps under review the Government's defence and overseas policy."

Ministerial Committee on Northern Ireland (IN): includes the Prime Minister (Chairman), the Deputy Prime Minister and First Secretary of State, the Chancellor of the Exchequer, the Secretary of State for the Home Department, the Secretary of State for Foreign and Commonwealth Affairs Secretary of State for Northern Ireland, the Lord Privy Seal, the Secretary of State for Defence, and the Attorney General; the Minister without Portfolio receives papers, while other Ministers are invited to attend as the nature of the business requires. It "oversees the Government's policy on Northern Ireland issues and relations with the Republic of Ireland on these matters."

Ministerial Committee on Intelligence Services (CSI): includes the Prime Minister (Chair), the Deputy Prime Minister and First Secretary of State, the Chancellor of the Exchequer, the

Secretary of State for Foreign and Commonwealth Affairs, the Secretary of State for the Home Department, and the Secretary of State for Defence. It "keeps under review policy on the security and intelligence services".

Ministerial Sub-Committee on Protective and Preventive Security (DOP (IT)(T)): includes the Secretary of State for the Home Department (Chair), the Secretary of State for Foreign and Commonwealth Affairs, the Secretary of State for Environment, Food and Rural Affairs, the Secretary of State for Health, the Secretary of State for Defence, the Secretary of State for Northern Ireland, the Chief Secretary, Treasury, and the Secretary of State for Trade and Industry. It "keeps under review the Government's policy on preventive precautionary security measures to counter the threat of terrorism in the United Kingdom and to British interests overseas: and to report to the Sub-Committee on International Terrorism as appropriate."

In addition, both the Ministerial Sub-Committee on European Issues (EP) and the World Summit on Sustainable Development (MISC18) have concern in this area.

The Cabinet Secretariat is non-departmental in function and purpose. It sits in the Cabinet Office, but serves the Prime Minister and Ministers who chair committees, rather than Cabinet Office Ministers themselves (except in their role as Committee Chairmen). The head of the Secretariat is the Secretary of the Cabinet (at present, Sir Richard Wilson). Overall, the Secretariat aims to ensure that properly-supported policy decisions area taken in a timely and efficient way. The Secretariat is composed of seven individual secretariats: Economic and Domestic; Defence and Overseas; European; Civil Contingencies; Central; Ceremonial; and the Joint Intelligence and Security Secretariat (comprising the Assessments Staff and Intelligence Support Secretariat) – these are responsible as follows:

The Economic and Domestic Secretariat deals with all domestic issues other than Lords Reform, Freedom of Information and Human Rights issues which are dealt with by the Central Secretariat. It also deals with legislative and Parliamentary matters. The European Secretariat is responsible for the co-ordination of EU business.

In addition to co-ordinating the formation of policy on a wide range of defence, security and foreign policy issues, the Defence and Overseas Secretariat is responsible for the co-ordination of the Government's response (military, economic and diplomatic) to crises overseas. A lot of this work is conducted through ad hoc committee arrangements.

The Central Secretariat assists the Secretary of the Cabinet in matters affecting the machinery of Government, propriety and relations with Parliament. The Ceremonial Secretariat is responsible for Honours policy work across Government and the preparation of the Prime Minister's half-yearly Honours List.

The Joint Intelligence and Security Secretariat assesses situations and issues of current concern on the basis of all sources of information and advises the Secretary of the Cabinet on the co-ordination of the intelligence machinery and its resources and programmes.
In any matters of security concern, the primary role of the Cabinet Office Security Division is to support the relevant Cabinet official committees in developing protective security policy – and is, thus, central to all matters in this area. This includes promoting best practice, issuing guidance and providing advice across government and to associated bodies. These responsibilities cover all aspects of protective security policy including personnel, physical, document, IT and communications security. The policy framework on protective security applies to all Government departments and agencies, and also to private sector contractors who have access to sensitive material, but each department and agency is responsible, under Ministerial direction, for maintaining its own security regime. The Security Division also supports the work of the National Infrastructure Security Co-ordination Centre (NISCC), the interdepartmental organisation set up to co-ordinate and develop existing work within Government departments and agencies, and organisations in the private sector, to defend The UK's critical infrastructure against electronic attack.

There are close links between the Secretariat and the No 10 Policy Directorate. These are needed in planning of business and the ensure that the Prime Minister's views are taken into account on business not coming before Cabinet or a Cabinet Committee he chairs.

The Civil Contingencies Secretariat

Central to all of these efforts is the Civil Contingencies Secretariat, which is responsible for improving The UK's resilience to disruptive challenges through anticipation, preparation, prevention and resolution. The CCS is part of the Cabinet Office; it was established in July 2001 (following the autumn 2000 fuel protests, the floods in the winter of 2000 and the outbreak of foot-and-mouth disease), and reports to the Prime Minister through the Cabinet Secretary. For any response to and for the purposes of emergency planning, the CCS is the central source of information, working with the lead government departments – the Home Office, the NHS, the Department for Transport, Local Government and the Regions and the Department of Trade and Industry, plus the military, police, other emergency services, and local authorities. Dissemination of public information, at local and national level, is a key part of the planning process.

In the field of civil protection, the CCS aims:

- To enhance the quality of national civil protection by taking a leading part in central government arrangements.
- To promote the safety of the public from disasters through enhancing the quality of local civil protection.

- To enhance the quality of national civil protection by promoting at an international level HM Government's interests in civil protection.

It is a co-ordinating body and centre of expertise set up to improve the resilience (defined as The UK's ability to handle disruptive challenges that can lead to or result in crisis) of Central Government and The UK. Like all Cabinet Office Secretariats, it supports Ministers collectively, servicing the Civil Contingencies Committee, which is chaired by the Home Secretary. Its purpose is to make the country more effective in planning for, dealing with and learning lessons from emergencies and disasters.
Its tasks are to identify potential crises; to help departments pre-empt them or handle them; and to manage any necessary co-ordination machinery. Its functions include some of the emergency planning responsibilities previously in the Home Office, but go considerably beyond them. The work includes the review of emergency planning legislation, which deals with the responsibilities of those involved in the local reactions. It also includes payment of grants to local authorities to support this work.

Officials from the CCS carry out the day-to-day executive, policy and representational work. The CCS is organised around five divisions:

- Assessment: an assessment function is being established within CCS to scan the horizon for major domestic disruptive challenges and to give advance warning of potential problems and their likely impact on the country. Though small, the Assessment Team will have a wide remit (all civil, non-terrorist, disruptive challenges to The UK). It will work closely with organisations across the public sector and beyond to learn about emerging problems and relevant interrelationships.
- Capability Management works with departments facing disruptive challenges. It will advise on crisis pre-emption or management processes; provide knowledge of where to find expertise, experience and resources; and help with planning when a challenge or crisis is faced. In the longer term, it will develop a resilience standard and manage an audit process for Government. Communication and Learning has two branches. One is the News Co-ordination Centre, which co-ordinates information for the public during a cross-departmental emergency working closely with Government Departments and non-Government partners. The second is the Emergency Planning College at Easingwold (Yorkshire), where the programme is to be developed as a key means of driving resilience and best practice across all sectors.
- The National Resilience Framework is the CCS division that works to develop key partnerships with and between all the communities of interest that can deliver resilience. These include local authorities, voluntary agencies, local communities and private sector groupings.

- Programme Co-ordination conducts risk management for the whole of the Secretariat. It supports the CCC and its sub committees; and manages the operations centre which co-ordinates the work of CCS, particularly during an emergency.

The Secretariat is also taking forward the review of emergency planning in England and Wales, which the Deputy Prime Minister announced after the fuel crisis and the floods in 2000. The review flows from the Government's conclusion that the Civil Defence Act 1948 no longer provides an adequate framework for emergency planning. A new framework is required. Because of that, a consultation exercise is now under way, and a consultation document was issued on 23 August 2001, which went to local authorities, chief constables, chief fire officers and various regulatory and professional bodies.

Following 11 September 2001, the terrorist attacks in the United States required a revision of the basic assumptions underlying British civil contingency planning arrangements, at all levels. The CCS is co-ordinating the work now underway to identify where it is necessary to revise and enhance our arrangements. CCS resilience work is focused on central government, London, and the essential elements of The UK's infrastructure. Its work covers both conventional and unconventional threats.

The London Resilience Committee

Under the CCC, the London Resilience Committee (chaired by Minister for London Nick Raynsford) includes the Mayor of London and representatives from London's key stakeholders in contingency planning such as the emergency services, local authorities, transport operators, NHS and utility companies. The Committee is supported by the London Resilience Team, composed of people from the organisations represented on the Committee who have first-hand experience in the key areas. These include the Metropolitan Police Service, British Transport Police, London Fire Brigade, London Ambulance Service, National Health Service, Mayor and Greater London Authority, Association of London Government, Corporation of the City of London Emergency Planning Department, London Underground, and Thames Water. The aim of the team is to make sure that the emergency plans and procedures of London organisations vital to keeping the capital running fit together effectively and can stand up to different scales and types of threat.

Finally, the **London Emergency Services Liaison Panel (LESP)** was established in 1973 and consists of representatives from the Metropolitan Police Service, the London Fire Brigade, City of London Police, British Transport Police, London Ambulance Service and local authorities. The group meets once every three months under the chair of the Metropolitan Police. Its purpose is to ensure a partnership approach between all the relevant agencies in the planning for, and the response to, a major incident of whatever kind. This could be anything from a terrorist attack to a natural disaster such as a severe flood, which may occur within the Greater London area.

UNSCR1373 Interdepartmental Group

The UK has also established an Interdepartmental Group To Oversee The Implementation Of UN Security Council Resolution 1373 (SCR 1373 – see below), which consists of representatives of the Foreign and Commonwealth Office, the Treasury, the Home Office, the Department of Trade and Industry, HM Customs and Excise, the Department for Transport and the Regions, and the Bank of England. The Group has met on a number of occasions to discuss support for the work of the CTC, the preparation of the United Kingdom's response to the CTC and possible ways of providing assistance to other States.

Agencies & Departments

Other government agencies and departments which play a role – further to the above – in any counter-terrorism efforts include the following.

The Security Service (MI5): The Security Service is The UK's security intelligence agency. Its purpose is to protect national security from threats such as terrorism, espionage and the proliferation of weapons of mass destruction, to safeguard the economic well-being of The UK against foreign threats, and to support the law enforcement agencies in preventing and detecting serious crime. The Security Service's key responsibility is for intelligence work to investigate and counter covertly organised threats. These include terrorism, espionage and the proliferation of weapons of mass destruction. In addition, it provides security advice to help reduce vulnerability to threats. In 1999, approximately 30.5% of its estimated £140 million budget was devoted to terrorism related to Northern Ireland, and 22.5% devoted to International Terrorism.

The Metropolitan Police Special Operations Branch (including the Anti-Terrorism Branch): The Metropolitan Police Service (MPS or "Met") has various specialist units that work across the capital or which fulfil a national role. A number of these are grouped into a section of the organisation known as Specialist Operations. They deal with tasks such as intelligence, security, protection of politicians, embassies and royalty, and the investigation of certain categories of serious crimes, including racial and violent crime and terrorism.

Under the Anti-Terrorist National Co-ordinator, the Anti-Terrorist Branch – also known as SO13 – is fully equipped to provide a 24-hour service, with teams of officers immediately available to respond to any type of incident or investigation. Senior investigating officers are supported by experienced detectives, forensic scene examiners, search trained personnel and surveillance officers. Other facilities include an extensive major incident room and research team. The Anti-Terrorist Branch responsibilities include:

- To investigate all acts of terrorism within the Metropolitan Police area including economic terrorism, politically motivated crimes, and some cases of kidnap and extortion
- To help with investigations in other areas of the country. The Commander of the Anti-Terrorist Branch is appointed by the Association of Chief Police Officers (ACPO) as the national co-ordinator for the investigation of acts of terrorism and cases involving animal rights extremism
- To take responsibility for prevention and planning as well as running counter-terrorist exercises for training and contingency planning purposes
- The Counter-Terrorist Search Wing advises generally on all aspects of specialist searches, with responsibility for the policy, training and licensing of search trained officers within the MPS
- To provide explosives officers within the MPS

Other branches of the Met SO Branch concerned with terrorism include Covert Operations (SO10) and Intelligence (SO11). Intelligence functions have been re-organised as part of the general re-structuring of Specialist Operations. SO11 has a broad responsibility for gathering, collating and analysing intelligence about criminal activity. SO10 has specific responsibility for covert operations.

Alongside the Met SO Branch Anti-Terrorism Branch is the National Terrorist Crime Prevention Unit (NTCPU). In addition, each THE UK Police Force has a Counter Terrorist Crime Prevention Officer who liases with the NTCPU.

Finally, the Met has set up a dedicated team of officers to investigate incidents in which suspect packages have been identified as hoaxes. The team consists of officers from the Serious Crime Group and they will work closely with the Crown Prosecution Service and the Anti-Terrorist Branch.

The National Infrastructure Security Co-ordination Centre (NISCC): an interdepartmental organisation set up to co-ordinate and develop existing work within Government departments and agencies and organisations in the private sector to defend the CNI against electronic attack. NISCC operates under a Director, who is a member of a Management Board chaired by the Home Office. The other members of the Board are drawn from the Cabinet Office, the Communications-Electronics Security Group (CESG) of GCHQ, the Security Service, the Ministry of Defence and the Police. NISCC's small core staff are from various parent departments contributing to the CNI protection programme. It co-ordinates a programme of work consisting of activity carried out by its core staff, and work carried out under the auspices of various government departments (but contributing directly or indirectly to the overall CNI programme). NISCC is responsible for co-ordinating: dialogue with owners of CNI systems to identify the most critical systems and work with them to reach a level of assurance about the protection of these systems; alerts or warnings of attack; assistance in response to serious attacks; information about the threat; and specialist protective security advice and expertise.

Other Agencies & Departments: Ministry of Defence, HM Customs & Excise, British Transport Police, THE UK Atomic Energy Authority. The Home Secretary also recently announced that, with the Chancellor of the Exchequer, he would be establishing a new anti-terrorist finance unit.

First Response To Disasters, Including Major Terrorist Incidents.

In order to achieve a combined and co-ordinated response to a major incident the capabilities of the emergency services must be closely linked with those of local authorities and other agencies. A national structure has been agreed and adopted which ensures that all involved parties understand their role in the combined response and how the differing levels of management arrangements inter-relate. The management framework which has been established embodies the same principles irrespective of the cause or nature of the incident, but remains flexible to individual circumstances. This framework:

- Allows each agency to tailor its own response plans to interface with the plans of others.
- Ensures all parties involved understand their role in the combined response.
- Explains how the differing levels of management arrangements relate to each other.
- Retains flexibility of option to suit local circumstances.

The management of the response can be divided into three levels: Operational, Tactical and Strategic. The requirement to implement one or more of these management levels will be very dependent on the nature of the incident, but normally incidents will be handled at the Operational level, only moving on to the Tactical and finally the Strategic level should this prove necessary.

In its planning, each agency will need to recognise the three management levels Operational, Tactical and Strategic and the functions to be undertaken. This will allow the integration of management processes across agency boundaries. It is not intended that the management levels necessarily predetermine the rank or seniority of the individual discharging the functions. If any one agency activates its major incident plans then it may be necessary for others to start to activate their own plans in order to facilitate liaison.

It is a characteristic of the command and control chain that it tends to be created from the bottom up. At the start of any incident for which there has been no warning the Operational level will be activated first, with the other levels coming into being with the escalation of the incident or a greater awareness of the situation.

Operational Level: On arrival at the scene of an event, the emergency services will take appropriate immediate measures and assess the extent of the problem, under the command of their respective Incident Officers. They will concentrate on their specific tasks within their areas of responsibility and act on delegated responsibility from their parent organisations until other levels of command are established. All this takes place at the Operational level and is the normal day-to-day arrangement for responding to any incident. The command of the resources belonging to any agency and applied within a geographical area, or used for a specific purpose, will be retained by that agency. Each agency must liaise fully and continually with others employed within the same area to ensure an efficient and combined effort. Where appropriate, the police will normally act as the co-ordinator of this response at the scene. These arrangements will usually be adequate for the effective resolution of most incidents. However, for more serious incidents - requiring significantly greater resources - it may be necessary to implement an additional level of management.

Tactical Level: Tactical level of management is introduced in order to determine priority in allocating resources, to plan and co-ordinate when a task will be undertaken, and to obtain other resources as required.

Most, but not all, of the Tactical functions will be discharged at or close to the scene of the incident. Some agencies, particularly local authorities, will prefer to operate from their administrative offices but will normally send a liaison officer to the scene to liase with the Incident Officer(s). Planning must also take into account that there may be a number of individual scenes, or in fact no actual scene to attend, for example where the incident is overseas.

When more than one agency is operating at the Tactical level there must be consultation between the various agency Incident Officers. The Tactical Commanders should not become involved with the activities at the scene being discharged by Incident Officers, but concentrate on the overall general management. In order to effect co-ordination, an inter agency meeting should be held at regular intervals attended by each Tactical Commander and normally chaired by the police. Liaison officers from the local authority should attend and other agencies such as the transport police or utilities may be invited to attend.

If it becomes apparent that resources, or expertise beyond the level of the Tactical Commander is required, or should there be the need to co-ordinate more than one incident/scene (where tactical command has been established), it may be necessary to implement a Strategic level of management.

Strategic Level: The purpose of the Strategic level of management is to establish a framework of policy within which Tactical Commanders will work, to give support to the Tactical Commander(s) by the provision of resources, to give consideration to the prioritisation of demands from any number of Incident Officers and to determine plans for the return to a state of normality once the incident is brought under control. The requirement for strategic management may be confined to one particular agency. However, certain incidents require a multi-agency response at the Strategic level in order to effect resolution. In such incidents a Strategic Co-ordinating Group should be formed.

The Strategic Co-ordinating Group: It will normally be a police responsibility to establish and chair the Strategic Co-ordinating Group (SCG). However, due to the nature of some major incidents other agencies may wish to initiate its formation and chair the group, e.g. for a rabies threat. Chairmanship may at some stage be passed to another agency (e.g. from the police to the local authority to manage the recovery phase). The SCG is normally made up from a nominated senior member from each statutory agency involved with the response. Each person must be able to make executive decisions in respect of resources within their agency and have the authority to seek the aid of other agencies in support of their role. The SCG provides the focus for communication to and from the Lead Government Department. Depending on the nature of the incident, government advisors or liaison officers may attend meetings, such as for nuclear or terrorist incidents.

The SCG will need to take account of the features of the particular incident, together with the professional expertise of each of the agencies and their statutory duties. On occasions it may be necessary to assign the control of specific functions to one or more of the agencies. In extreme circumstances, such as a terrorist incident, it may be necessary for the police to take executive action in respect of the total incident. The SCG should be aware of its wider role which may encompass central government interests, handling requests for advice and assistance from individual services and agencies, and media demands. In the event of widespread disaster the SCG will need to liaise with similar neighbouring SCGs and, during the recovery phase, with the appropriate Government Office of the Region. The SCG should develop a strategy for dealing with the media, designate a media briefing centre and appoint a media briefing centre manager (normally a police press officer). The SCG should be based at an appropriate pre-planned location, away from the noise and confusion of the scene. It is usual to locate the SCG at Police Headquarters, but this may move to the local authority during the recovery phase when the emergency services may have little or no involvement.

Selected elements of national policymaking and implementation

Either in place prior to 11 September 2001 or in reaction to the events of 11 September 2001, The UK government has put forward the following initiatives.

Legislative Action

Before 11 September – and particularly until 2000 – the United Kingdom had a wide range of legislative measures in place to counteract terrorist activity. The centrepiece of this legislative framework was the Terrorism Act 2000. Other relevant legislation included the Immigration Act 1971, the Customs and Excise Management Act 1979, the Extradition Act 1989 and the Export of Goods (Control) Order 1994.

Most particularly, these instruments outlined terrorist offences as including (Annex C: The Suppression of Terrorism Act 1978 Schedule 1- List of Offences): murder; manslaughter or culpable homicide; rape; kidnapping; abduction or plagium; false imprisonment; assault occasioning actual bodily harm or causing injury; and wilful fire-raising. These were broken-down into:

- Offences against the person (under the Offences against the Person Act 1861) covered section 4 (soliciting etc to commit murder); section 18 (wounding with intent to cause grievous bodily harm); section 20 (causing grievous bodily harm); section 21 (attempting to choke etc in order to commit or assist in the committing of any indictable offence); section 22 (using chloroform etc to commit or assist in the committing of any indictable offence); section 23 (maliciously administering poison etc so as to endanger life or inflict grievous bodily harm); section 24 (maliciously administering poison etc with intent to injure etc); and section 48 (rape).
- Abduction was covered (under the Offences against the Person Act 1861) for section 55 (abduction of unmarried girl under 16); and section 56 (child-stealing or receiving stolen child) – in addition, section 20 of the Sexual Offences Act 1956 covered abduction of unmarried girl under 16.
- Taking of hostages (under the Taking of Hostages Act 1982) included an offence under section 2 of the Child Abduction Act 1984 (abduction of child by person other than parent etc) or any corresponding provision in force in Northern Ireland.
- Explosives use was covered (under the Offences against the Person Act 1861) for section 28 (causing bodily injury by gunpowder); section 29 (causing gunpowder to explode etc with intent to grievous bodily harm); section 30 (placing gunpowder near a building etc with intent to cause bodily injury) – as well as (under the Substances Act 1883) section 2 (causing explosion likely to endanger life or property); and section 3 (doing any act with intent to cause such explosion, conspiring to cause such an explosion, or making or possessing explosive with intent to endanger life or property).
- Nuclear materials were covered under any provision of the Nuclear Material (Offences) Act 1983.
- Firearms were covered (under the Firearms Act 1968) for an offence under section 16 (possession of firearm with to injure); and an offence under subsection (1) of section 17 (use of firearm or imitation firearm to resist arrest) involving the use attempted use of a firearm within the meaning of that section. In addition, the Firearms (Northern Ireland) Order 1981 covered an offence under Article 17 consisting of a person's in his possession any firearm or ammunition (within the meaning that Article) with intent by means thereof to endanger life, or to enable another person by means thereof to endanger life; and an offence under paragraph (1) of Article 18(use of firearm or imitation firearm to resist arrest) involving the use or attempted use of a firearm within the meaning of that Article.
- Offences against property were covered under section 1(2) of the Criminal Damage Act 1971 (destroying or damaging property intending to endanger life or being reckless as to danger to life), as well as Article 3(2) of the Criminal Damage (Ireland)

Order 1977 (destroying or damaging property intending to endanger life or being reckless as to danger to life).

- Offences in relation to aircraft were covered under Part I of the Aviation Security Act 1982 (other than an offence under section 4 or 7 of that Act), as well as under section 1 of the Aviation and Maritime Security Act 1990. In addition, all offences relating to ships and fixed platforms were covered under Part II of the Aviation and Maritime Security Act 1990 (other than an offence under section 15 of that Act), and Part II of the Channel Tunnel (Security) Order 1994 No 570 which covered Channel Tunnel trains and the tunnel system.
- Finally, the financing of terrorism (considered in more depth below) was covered under any of sections 15 to 18 of the Terrorism Act 2000.

In 2000, the government introduced – as its centrepiece of this legislative framework – the Terrorism Act 2000, which updated a number of the above instruments and ensured that proper definitions of activities and actors was in place in this regard. The Terrorism Act 2000 came into force on 19 February 2001. This new permanent legislation, which is the responsibility of the Home Secretary, applies to foreign as well as domestic terrorist groups. The Act demonstrates the United Kingdom Government's commitment to supporting the international community in the fight against international terrorism. The purpose of the act is to help the police and prosecuting authorities take effective action against those concerned in terrorism. It is not intended, and will not be used to restrict genuine freedom of speech and will not be used to curb lawful support for political opposition or change. Such rights are longstanding and valued in The UK and are protected by the European Convention on Human Rights.

The Home Secretary has the power to add or remove organisations from the list at any time. A proscribed organisation may apply to the Home Secretary to be de-proscribed. Appeals against refusal to de-proscribe will be considered by an independent commission. The Home Secretary has published a list of foreign terrorist organisations to be added to those groups concerned in terrorism in Northern Ireland already proscribed in the Act. Proscription of these organisations under the Terrorism Act 2000 took effect on 28 March 2001.

Therefore, before 11 September, the United Kingdom had a wide range of legislative measures in place to counteract terrorist activity. Following the events of 11 September, it was decided to enhance The UK's existing Anti-Terrorism legislation – resulting in the Anti-Terrorism, Crime and Security Act 2001 which received royal assent on 14 December 2001. Legislation has also been adopted under the United Nations Act 1946. Finally, the Terrorism Act 2000 (Proscribed Organisations) (Amendment) Order 2001 also introduced additions to the Proscribed Organisations listed in the Terrorism Act 2000.

The Anti-Terrorism, Crime and Security Act 2001 included measures for:

- Tough financial controls to staunch the flow of terrorist funding
- Powers for account monitoring and swift asset freezing, seizure of cash in-country, and strict reporting obligations on the financial sector including making it an offence for a bank not to report a transaction where it knows or suspects funds may be intended for terrorist purposes;
- Measures to allow quicker and more effective co-operation with fellow EU countries on police and legal issues;
- An extension of the incitement law to cover religious, as well as racial hatred. Both incitement offences will have an increased maximum penalty from two years to seven years;
- Widening of the incitement law to cover incitement within The UK of terrorist acts against groups or individuals overseas and examining additional powers in relation to conspiracy;
- A requirement on transport companies to keep passenger and freight information records and make them available in advance to law enforcement agencies;
- The removal of current barriers which prevent customs and revenue officers providing information to law enforcement agencies in their fight against terrorism;
- Measures to enable communication service providers to retain data generated in the course of their business, namely the records of calls made and other data - not the content. Government will work with the industry on a Code of Practice to take this forward;
- The strengthening of security at airports and for passengers. Powers both within restricted areas at airports and aboard aircraft will all be strengthened;
- Expanding the role and jurisdiction of the British Transport Police, together with those working on enforcement from the Ministry of Defence and the Atomic Energy Authority. Their powers will be widened beyond the boundaries of particular sites.
- Powers to give the police and customs services the authority to demand the removal of facial covering or gloves;
- Clauses to close the gaps in our present legislation relating to chemical, nuclear and biological weapons to prevent the use, production, possession or participation in unauthorised transfers of these materials;
- Fingerprints taken in immigration and asylum cases can be retained for up to 10 years in order to improve identification of individuals.

The Act also contains robust and streamlined procedures for dealing with those suspected of terrorist acts who seek to misuse our asylum and immigration systems. These measures will:

- Remove access to judicial review in decisions made by the Special Immigration Appeals Commission, the body that deals with suspected terrorists' asylum claims;
- Enable asylum claims to be rejected where the Secretary of State certifies the person is a threat to national security; and

- Detain those who are a terrorist threat but who cannot be removed from the country, whilst retaining a right of appeal. This will require a limited suspension from Article 5 of the ECHR, using ECHR Article 15 which allows for suspension in the event of a public emergency. This will ensure we remain consistent with our international obligations, including the 1951 Geneva Convention on refugees.

In addition, provisions to detain suspected international terrorists who pose a threat to national security, but cannot currently be removed from The UK, would be subject to a new Act of Parliament after five years. Such detention provisions are intended to prevent the abuse of THE UK immigration and asylum laws by terrorists: these measures would address the problem faced where someone could be deported under existing powers, but no safe country can be immediately found.

In addition, the Proceeds of Crime Bill was introduced at the House of Commons on 18 October 2001 and contains measures to remove illegally-gained assets from criminals, including terrorists.

In the May 2002 budget, the Government announced increases of £87m for counter-terrorism this year, the bulk of which will go to the Metropolitan Police. This will cover:

- £49m for the Metropolitan Police including funding to cover the Golden Jubilee costs; (The Met receives a total of £62 million from the overall settlement). Depending on deployment decisions, in the Met, for example, this could provide for up to 700 new police officers and 460 community support officers over this financial year.
- £14m for other forces including an extra £2m for Greater Manchester ensuring an overall total of an additional £5 million Home Office funding for the Commonwealth Games security; and
- £24m for a range of other counter-terrorism measures.

The Government also implemented a scheme to provide insurance cover for THE UK airlines in the wake the 11 September attacks; it expired on 23 January 2002. Airlines and service providers will be required to find commercial cover for the first 50 mln Euro of third party war and terrorism liabilities. The Government-backed Troika scheme will provide the cover for liabilities above those minimum levels. Premiums will be payable by all airlines covered by the Troika scheme. These will continue to be on the per passenger basis recommended in European Commission guidelines.

Confronting the Financing of Terrorism

In respect of the prevention and suppression of the financing of terrorist acts, the United Kingdom moved quickly to freeze the assets of those involved in the financing of terrorism following adoption of SCR 1373(2001). Lists were issued on 12 October, 2 November and 7

November 2001 identifying 48 individuals and 77 organisations whose accounts would be frozen pursuant to SCR 1373. These lists included individuals listed by the US under President Bush's Executive Order; the US list of 22 most wanted terrorists; the list of United Kingdom proscribed terrorist organisations; and the individuals and organisations listed by the United States on 7 November 2001. Those lists have been communicated to some 600 banks and other financial institutions in the United Kingdom, and have been published in a Bank of England Press Release.

In respect of existing offences and penalties with respect to such funding activities, the Terrorism Act 2000 describes four main offences in relation to terrorist funding:

- Fund raising: it is an offence to invite anyone to provide money or property; receive money or property; or provide money or property for the purposes of terrorism.
- Use and possession of money or property for the purposes of terrorism.
- Funding arrangements: involvement in arrangements whereby money or property is made available for terrorism.
- Money laundering: facilitating the retention or control of terrorist property in any way, including concealment; removal from the jurisdiction; and transfer to nominees.

All of these apply in situations where a person intends, or has reasonable cause to suspect, that money or property will be used for the purposes of terrorism. The maximum penalty for each of these offences is 14 years imprisonment, a fine, or both. There is also an obligation to disclose knowledge or suspicion of terrorist funding, based on information arising from one's trade, profession, business or employment. Failure to disclose such information is an offence subject to penalties of up to five years imprisonment, a fine or both. The Anti-Terrorism, Crime And Security Act 2001 adds a further offence to the Terrorism Act 2000 for those working in the regulated financial sector of failing to disclose where there are reasonable grounds to suspect an offence under sections 15-18 of the 2000 Act has been committed.

In respect of existing legislation and procedures for freezing accounts and assets at banks and financial institutions that relate to terrorist, paragraph 1(c) of SCR 1373 is implemented in the United Kingdom by an Order in Council (SI 2001 No. 3365), made under section 1 of the United Nations Act 1946. This Order, which became effective on 10 October 2001, empowers the Treasury to direct banks and financial institutions to freeze the accounts of individuals and entities suspected of involvement in terrorism. Failure to do so is an offence. Since the adoption of SCR 1373, seven accounts have been frozen containing £7.2 million. Prior to the making of SI 2001 No. 3365, accounts in the United Kingdom of those associated with the Taliban and Usama bin Laden were frozen in accordance with the orders made pursuant to UNSCR 1267 and 1333, which are still in force. Parallel legislation has been adopted for the Crown Dependencies and Overseas Territories.

In the autumn of 2001, The UK – in co-ordination with international partners – circulated a list of 46 organisations and 16 individuals to financial institutions requiring that assets belonging to them be frozen. As of the end of November 2001, the total amount of assets frozen in The UK stood at £77 million in 38 accounts. The individuals and organisations named on the list are believed to have committed or pose a significant risk of committing or providing material support for acts of terrorism.

As of April 2002, The UK Government has fully met the commitments set out in the November 2001 IMFC Communiqué:
The UK has fully implemented C UNSCR 1373 (Terrorism) and C UNSCR 1267 (Taliban), UNSCR 1333 (Usama bin Laden) and 1390 (Taliban/UBL). Acting under the Terrorism (UN Measures) Order 2001 and the Al-Qaeda and Taliban (UN Measures) Order 2002, The UK has frozen the assets of over 100 organisations and over 200 individuals. A complete list of all those listed can be found at the Bank of England website.

The Anti-Terrorism, Crime and Security Act 2001 provides:

- Police powers to seize terrorist cash anywhere in The UK
- Police powers to freeze funds at the outset of investigation
- Police powers to monitor accounts which may be used to facilitate terrorism
- Tougher obligations on people to report suspicions that funds are destined for terrorism

The UK took effective action to freeze funds soon after UNSCRs 1267 and 1333 were adopted. Before 11 September, some $90 million of Taliban assets had been frozen; since 11 September some $10 million has been frozen. Efforts are now underway to return the bulk of these assets – around $85million – to the new legitimate Government in Kabul. Some $15million remains frozen.

A founder member of the Egmont Group, The UK established an Economic Crime Unit within its National Criminal Intelligence Service (NCIS) in 1992. A multi-agency Terrorist Finance Team was set up in NCIS in November 2001. NCIS hosts the Egmont Secretariat.
The UK continues to support the provision of technical assistance and capacity building in a number of countries, funding programmes and initiatives designed to address a range of anti-money laundering, anti-terrorist financing and other counter-terrorism issues. This funding is provided both bilaterally, and through contributions to multi-lateral initiatives.

THE UK banks and financial institutions have co-operated fully, constructively and with dedication in seeking out sources of terrorist funding.

The UK has introduced a new domestic regulatory regime to ensure that money-laundering regulations are implemented effectively by bureaux de change and money transmitters. The UK plays a significant role in FATF and already complies with the great majority of the Special 8 FATF Recommendations, and will soon be fully compliant following the passage of new regulations dealing with wire transfers by money remitters. The UK strongly supports international co-operation, enhanced mutual understanding and effective means of tackling terrorist financing. THE UK Overseas Territories and Crown Dependencies are fully committed to act in parallel with The UK in combating terrorist financing. They apply the UN Resolutions and are working to meet the Special 8 FATF Recommendations. The Financial Action Task Force (FATF) issued 8 Special Recommendations on Terrorist Financing on 30 October 2001. All FATF members, including The UK, are committed to implementing those Recommendations. The FATF is assessing compliance, and issued a questionnaire to all members before Christmas, with a follow-up in February 2001. Non-FATF members were asked to engage in the assessment process on a similar basis to FATF members, and the questionnaire has been issued to non-members with a request that it be completed by 1 May 2002.

Investigation and prosecution of terrorist crimes

The Metropolitan Police Service (MPS) is giving the FBI every support and assistance. The terrorist attack of 11 September has led to the largest terrorist investigation by the MPS outside The UK. A total of move than 5000 actions have been generated. Examples of such include:

- Yasser Al-Siri has been charged with conspiracy to murder in connection with the assassination of General Masoud.
- Sulayman Balal Zainulabidin has been charged under the Terrorism Act 2000 in connection with the provision of paramilitary training.
- Sheik Abdullah el-Faisal has been charged with encouraging others to murder.
-

Regional and International Responses

The unanimous adoption of Security Council Resolution 1373(2001) (SCR 1373)[82] on 28 September 2001 was an historic event. This was the first resolution to impose obligations on all states to respond to the global threat of terrorism. The UK played a leading part in securing a powerful Security Council Resolution that requires all member states to take effective action against terrorists: indeed, the UN's Counter-Terrorism Committee (CTC) is chaired by The UK Permanent Representative to the UN, Sir Jeremy Greenstock. The UK submitted its report to the Counter-Terrorism Committee on 19 December. This set out the steps taken by The UK to implement UN Security Council Resolution 1373 on counter-terrorism measures. The United Kingdom has taken a full range of legislative and executive measures to ensure compliance

[82] www.UN.org/Docs/scres/2001/res1373e.pdf

with SCR 1373, and is fully committed to the work of the CTC in ensuring global implementation of this resolution.

The CTC will also need to work closely with other international actors who are involved in the fight against terrorism, including the Vienna-based UN organisations, the International Financial institutions, regional organisations such as the EU and the OIC, the OECD and the G8 (including the Financial Action Task Force – FATF). The UK has actively promoted the work of the CTC in all these organisations and encouraged them to co-ordinate closely to prevent the waste of scarce human and financial resources.

Different Threats: NBCI

Government action in the area of Nuclear, Biological, Chemical and Infrastructure Terrorism since 11 September includes a number of initiatives. The most notable of these is Part 6 of the Anti-Terrorism, Crime and Security Act 2001 which strengthens current legislation controlling chemical, nuclear and biological weapons of mass destruction. It makes it an offence to aid or abet the overseas use or development of chemical, nuclear, biological. It introduces offences equivalent to those in the Chemical Weapons Act 1996 in relation to biological and nuclear weapons. This brings legislation on biological and nuclear weapons into line with existing legislation on chemical weapons. These provisions will cover nuclear and radiological weapons, chemical weapons and biological agents and toxins. There is also a new provision for customs and excise to prosecute.

Nuclear

All nuclear concerns are handled by The UK Atomic Energy Agency as the lead agency responsible. Part 8 of the Anti-Terrorism, Crime and Security Act 2001 ("Security Of Nuclear Industry") includes provisions for extending the jurisdiction for the United Kingdom Atomic Energy Authority Constabulary (THE UKAEAC) so that it can protect nuclear sites and nuclear material more effectively. The provisions enable these constables to be deployed to all civil licensed nuclear sites, rather than as at present only on premises of specified nuclear operators, and within five kilometres of such sites. The provisions also provide for regulations to be made to reinforce and update the regulatory regime for security in the civil nuclear industry. In addition, they strengthen sanctions against the unauthorised disclosure by individuals of sensitive information on the security of nuclear sites, nuclear material and proliferation-sensitive nuclear technology.

The UK Government has also recently backed international efforts to combat nuclear terrorism with a £250,000 contribution to a fund run by the International Atomic Energy Agency (IAEA), which will support activities aimed at combating nuclear terrorism. The IAEA has reviewed its activities and has strengthened its work to assist Member States to protect against acts of terrorism involving nuclear and other radioactive materials. The funding will be used by the IAEA on a number of activities, including:

- Nuclear security related training
- Funding International Physical Protection Advisory Service missions which provide Member-States with advice on their legal and regulatory infrastructure and the implementation of physical protection arrangements
- Preparing guidance and materials aimed at helping IAEA Member-States improve their legal and regulatory structures
- Developing good State Systems of Accountancy and Control to improve the proper accountancy for nuclear materials

Biological & Chemical

Review of all plans for protecting the public from any possible biological or chemical attack by the Chief Medical Officer. Ensuring Doctors know how to access information from the Public Health Laboratory Service website on the signs and symptoms of anthrax. Signing of an agreement with the United States on protecting citizens from bio-terrorism through the pooling of intelligence, expertise and planning. Securing additional supplies of drugs and equipment for use in an emergency. Extensive contingency planning is in place based on guidance that was issued by the Government to the NHS last year. New guidance has also been issued and the Government plans to update this information.

In February 2002, The UK's fire services were given £53 million in new funding to give further protection to the public and emergency services in the event of a major chemical, biological or radiological attack. The funding would provide new equipment, including decontamination facilities for members of the public and personal protective equipment for fire-fighters.

Infrastructure

All activities and concerns relating to the Critical National Infrastructure (CNI) are tasked foremost to the National Infrastructure Security Co-ordination Centre (NISCC). NISCC also houses the Unified Incident Reporting and Alert Scheme (UNIRAS) which draws on technical support from CESG, The UK national technical security authority. While its original customers were government departments and agencies, this has recently been expanded to include companies holding sensitive Government contracts, and most recently CNI organisations. It:

- Receives reports of significant electronic attack incidents, threats, new vulnerabilities and countermeasures from its customer base and other commercial, Government and international sources. It then validates, sanitises (where appropriate) and disseminates the information back to its customers through e-mail alerts and warnings.
- Provides a helpdesk for its customers, giving advice on IT security incidents, particularly Internet-related problems;
- Co-ordinates the NISCC's Electronic Attack Response Group (EARG), which responds to serious electronic attack incidents affecting the CNI;

- Is The UK Government CERT (Computer Emergency Response Team) and is an active member of the international Forum of Incident Response and Security Teams (FIRST);
- Collates reports on IT security incidents supplied by its customers and issues regular statistics.

Europe

The United Kingdom has always participated actively in counter-terrorism action within the EU and will continue to do so. The special European Council on 20 and 21 September 2001 agreed that counter-terrorism should be a priority for the Union, both internally and in its relations with third countries. Heads of State and Government endorsed an EU Action Plan on 21 September to help member States step up the fight against global terrorism and to improve practical co-operation among member States. To date, 68 concrete measures under the Action Plan have been identified and taken forward. These measures include:

- Creation of fast-track extradition and an EU arrest warrant, which should significantly reduce obstacles to extradition within EU;
- Agreement on common EU offences and penalties for terrorist activity;
- Setting up a team of EU Member States' anti-terrorist experts who can ensure timely collection and analysis of information and intelligence and draft threat assessments;
- Conclusion of the US/Europol agreement on 6 December;
- The rapid implementation of the UN Convention for the Suppression of the Financing of Terrorism by all EU Member States;
- A requirement that the potential impact on the fight against crime and terrorism is fully considered in the drafting EC legislation;
- Measures on freezing of assets and evidence;
- A review of the EU's relations with third countries in the light of their support for counter-terrorism.

On 10 December, the Council of the EU agreed a Common Position and Regulation to implement the UNSCR 1373 provision relating to the suppression of terrorist financing. In addition, The UK would aim to further support the recent agreements signed between the United States and the European Union which aim to build on the solid co-operation already achieved by dealing with extradition matters and improving the exchange of intelligence and law enforcement information, including the US-EU Europol initial co-operation agreement of December 2001 which aims to facilitate co-operation on serious international crimes such as terrorism; and the activities of the European Commission's Political & Security Committee (PSC), especially for intelligence purposes.

The UK has also pushed the EU to confirm its counter-terrorism measures by adopting tough penalties to fight terrorism and the widest possible scope for the European Arrest Warrant, ensuring that these have maximum impact in the fight against terrorism. Measures to support this co-ordinated counter-terrorism policy would include:

- Better EU law enforcement structures;
- Stronger action against drugs;
- Quick progress towards a common European asylum system and tough action to combat illegal immigration and human trafficking; and
- A renewed commitment to mutual recognition as the basis for international judicial co-operation.

Action in the Overseas Territories and Crown Dependencies

The UK is responsible for the international relations of its Overseas Territories and Crown Dependencies. Three Overseas Territories (Bermuda, Gibraltar and the Cayman Islands) have indicated that they will apply the relevant provisions of the Terrorism Act 2000 and the Anti-Terrorism, Crime and Security Act by local legislation. The remaining Overseas Territories have opted for the United Kingdom to do so on their behalf, through an Order in Council. A first draft of the Overseas Territories model legislation will be ready in early January 2002, for consultation with the Overseas Territories shortly thereafter. The Government hopes that the Overseas Territories will, by Spring 2002 be in a position to (a) bring the necessary legislation to their local legislature for approval (in the cases of Cayman, Bermuda, Gibraltar), or (b) agree that the United Kingdom should make an Order In Council on their behalf (for the remainder). The Crown Dependencies (the Channel Islands and the Isle of Man) are introducing their own domestic legislation to apply measures equivalent to those in the United Kingdom's Terrorism Act 2000 and the Anti-Terrorism Crime and Security Act 2001. Action in relation to the to the Overseas Territories and Crown Dependencies has also been taken under the United Nations Act 1946 (through SI Numbers 3363, 3364 and 3366).

International Co-ordination & Co-operation

Technical Assistance to Other States: The United Kingdom has a wide-ranging programme of bilateral assistance in counter-terrorism, aimed at preventing terrorism, apprehending terrorists and contributing to stability and preventing conflicts. In the past five years, activities covered by this programme have included visits, seminars and training projects in hostage negotiations; explosive and ordinance disposal; aviation and maritime transport security; bomb scene management; and crisis management.

The United Kingdom also supports the establishment of a Global Trust Fund to provide technical assistance to countries that need help in implementing SCR 1373. This could cover advice on drafting relevant legislation; assessment of precise needs for training; advice on protective security measures; and training and advice for financial control authorities. The CTC has already done much valuable work in collating information on what expertise, including from The UK, is already available in these areas. The United Kingdom would be willing to make a significant contribution to such a fund should it be established.

Ending Terrorist Financing: The UK will also support the November 2001 Finance Action Task Force international standards to combat terrorist financing. Recommendations include: criminalising the financing of terrorism, powers to freeze and confiscate terrorist assets, and obligatory reporting requirements on financial institutions. The recommendations the Task Force has agreed to adopt will ensure that all OECD member countries introduce regulations as comprehensive as those that are already in place in The UK. The Special Recommendations on Terrorist Financing – which must be in place by 30 June 2002 – will commit members to:

- Take immediate steps to ratify and implement the relevant United Nations instruments.
- Criminalise the financing of terrorism, terrorist acts and terrorist organisations.
- Freeze and confiscate terrorist assets.
- Report suspicious transactions linked to terrorism.
- Provide the widest possible range of assistance to other countries' law enforcement and regulatory authorities for terrorist financing investigations.
- Impose anti-money laundering requirements on alternative remittance systems.
- Strengthen customer identification measures in international and domestic wire transfers.
- Ensure that entities, in particular non-profit organisations, cannot be misused to finance terrorism.

Conclusions

The UK has long dealt with the spectre of terrorism domestically – due largely but not exclusively to Irish-originating terrorism, as well as similar concerns in Scotland – as well as being a key participant in international efforts (whether military or otherwise) to counter and defeat terrorism. The institutions and legislation that it has in place currently is simply a reflection of that long concern growing in light of both the evolution of transnational terrorism into the 21st Century and the concerns specific to Al Qaeda that exist. In this sense, while the events of 9/11 may have increased the concerns and challenges presented by transnational terrorism, The UK Government believes strongly that it has a long-standing appreciation for and means to counter-terrorism that go beyond immediate reactions to 9/11.

Matrix of The United Kingdom's challenges, measures, actors, stages and progress

CHS: Challenges as outlined
Msrs: Measures 1-Strategic, 2-Operational, 3-Tactical
Actors: 1-Public sector, federal/national level, civil (including special forces), 2-Public sector, 3-Regional/state level, civil, 4-Public sector, local level, civil, 5-Military, 6-Private sector
Sgs: Stages: 1-pre-attack, 2-trans-attack, 3-post-attack
Pgs: Progress: 1-No specific post 9/11 action; 2-Need for action identified, policy in the making; 3-Budget appropriated, actors identified; 4-Policy implementation well underway; 5-Policy implementation finalised

Nr	Description UK post 9/11 policy making and -implementation	Categorisation				Remarks	Pgs
		Chs	Msrs	Ars	Sgs		
	ADMINISTRATION & GOVERNMENTAL ISSUES						
	Enhancement of existing high-level inter-ministerial and civil service working-group for co-ordinating the measures of various governmental bodies on a/c terrorism		1	1-5		Ministerial Committee on Civil Contingencies & COBRA Working Group	5
	Permanent intensified co-operation between ministries on matters concerning a/c terrorism		1,2	1-5		Via Civil Contingencies Secretariat/Cabinet Office	5
	LEGISLATIVE ISSUES						
	Existing anti-terrorist legislation pre-9/11						
	General anti-terrorist measures		1,2,3	All		Terrorism Act 2000 (updating Prevention of Terrorism Act 1978, in addition to other statutes)	1
	Existing four main offences in relation to terrorist funding: 1. Fund raising: it is an offence to invite anyone to provide money or property; receive money or property; or provide money or property for the purposes of terrorism. 2. Use and possession of money or property for the purposes of terrorism. 3. Funding arrangements: involvement in arrangements whereby money or property is made available for terrorism. 4. Money laundering: facilitating the retention or control of terrorist property in any way, including concealment; removal from the jurisdiction; and transfer to nominees		2,3	1-4, 6		Terrorism Act 2000	1
	Existing anti-terrorist legislation against "offences against the person"	1	3	1-5		Offences against the Person Act 1861	1
	Existing anti-terrorist legislation against "abduction"	1	3	1-5		Offences against the Person Act 1861; Sexual Offences Act 1956	1
	Existing anti-terrorist legislation against "taking of hostages"	1	3	1-5		Taking of Hostages Act 1982; Child Abduction Act 1984	1
	Existing anti-terrorist legislation against "explosives use"	3	3	1-5		Offences against the Person Act 1861; Substances Act 1883	1
	Existing anti-terrorist legislation relating to "nuclear materials"	4,6	3	1-5		Nuclear Material (Offences) Act 1983	1
	Existing anti-terrorist legislation relating to "firearms"	1,3	3	1-5		Firearms Act 1968; Firearms (Northern Ireland) Order 1981	1
	Existing anti-terrorist legislation against "offences against property"	5	3	1-5		Criminal Damage Act 1971; Criminal Damage (Ireland) Order 1977	1
	Existing anti-terrorist legislation against "offences relating to aircraft"	All	3	1-5		Aviation Security Act 1982; Aviation and Maritime Security Act 1990	1
	Existing anti-terrorist legislation against "offences relating to ships and fixed platforms"	All	3	1-5		Aviation and Maritime Security Act 1990; Channel Tunnel (Security) Order	1

					1994	
	Existing anti-terrorist legislation against "financing of terrorism"		3	1-5	Terrorism Act 2000	1
Anti-terrorism measures post-9/11						
	Review of existing legislation and introduction of amendments		1	1-2	Terrorism Act 2000; Terrorism Act 2000 (Proscribed Organisations) (Amendment) Order 2001	5
	Introduction of new legislation to extend law enforcement & national security powers to combat terrorism domestically		1	1-5	Anti-Terrorism, Crime and Security Act 2001	5
	Review of support for UN conventions on terrorism, especially in light of UNSCR-1373 and new UK legislation		1	1-2	Esp: Convention for the Suppression of Terrorist Bombings; Convention for the Suppression of the Financing of Terrorism	5
	Full support for and implementation of UNSCR-1373 (Terrorism), UNSCR-1267 (Taliban), UNSCR-1333 (Usama bin Laden), and UNSCR-1390 (Taliban/UBL) – including establishment of an Interdepartmental Group To Oversee The Implementation Of UNSCR-1373		1	1	Domestically	5
	Review of support for existing EU anti-terrorism measures, including ratification of the EU Framework Decision on Terrorism and necessary modifications to national legislation		1	1	European Convention on the Suppression of Terrorism 1977	5
	Widening of the incitement law to cover incitement within the UK of terrorist acts against groups or individuals overseas and examining additional powers in relation to conspiracy	1,3	1	1	Anti-Terrorism, Crime and Security Act 2001	5
	Extending of the incitement law to cover religious, as well as racial hatred	1,3	1	1	Anti-Terrorism, Crime and Security Act 2001	5
	Measures to detain those who are a terrorist threat but who cannot be removed from the country, whilst retaining a right of appeal		1	1	Anti-Terrorism, Crime and Security Act 2001: requires a limited suspension from Article 5 of the ECHR, using ECHR Article 15 which allows for suspension in the event of a public emergency	5
	Enable asylum claims to be rejected where the Secretary of State certifies the person is a threat to national security		1	1-4	Anti-Terrorism, Crime and Security Act 2001	5
	Introduce measures to remove illegally-gained assets from criminals, including terrorists		1	1-4	Proceeds of Crime Bill introduced on 18 October 2001	5
LAW ENFORCEMENT, PREVENTION & NATIONAL SECURITY MEASURES						
Law Enforcement Measures						
	May 2002 budget increase of £87m for counter-terrorism this FY, the bulk of which will go to the Metropolitan Police		2,3	3-4	Met Police: £24m for a range of counter-terrorism measures	3-4
	Detention of foreign nationals suspected of involvement in terrorism		2,3	3-4	As mandated in Anti-Terrorism, Crime and Security Act 2001 and Terrorism Act 2000	4
	Establishment of Counter-Terrorism Committee under Association of Chief Police Officers of the UK (ACPO-UK)		1,2,3	1-4		5
	Expansion in number of law enforcement assets devoted to protection		1,2	1-4		4-5
	Law enforcement on maximum alert		1,2,3	1-5		5
	Intensified efforts to trace possible contacts of persons with organizations of concern		2,3	1-4		4
	Removal of current barriers which prevent customs and revenue officers providing information to law enforcement agencies in their fight against terrorism		2,3	1-4	Anti-Terrorism, Crime and Security Act 2001	4-5
	Expansion of the role and jurisdiction of the British Transport Police, together with those working on enforcement from the Ministry of Defence and the Atomic Energy Authority		1,2,3	1-4	Anti-Terrorism, Crime and Security Act 2001	5
	Establishment of a multi-agency Terrorist Finance Team in the National Criminal		1,2,3	1-4	Part of Egmont Group support. The UK established	5

	Intelligence Service (NCIS) in November 2001					an Economic Crime Unit within NCIS in 1992. NCIS hosts the Egmont Secretariat.	
	Protective Security Measures						
	Increased protection around US and other embassies	All	1,2,3	1-5	1		5
	Increased security along public areas	All	1,2,3	1-5	1		5
	Increased public surveillance, including via CCTV	All	1,2,3	1-5	1		5
	Aviation, Transportation and Maritime Security						
	Securing internal borders and airspace, including increased airspace surveillance	All	1,2,3	1-5	1		5
	Higher security level in the field of aviation	All	1,2,3	All	1		5
	Review of emergency plan for cases of aircraft hijackings	All	1,2,3	All	1		5
	Introduction of a requirement on transport companies to keep passenger and freight information records and make them available in advance to law enforcement agencies	All	2,3	All	1	Anti-Terrorism, Crime and Security Act 2001	5
	Intelligence & National Security Measures						
	Enhancing internal intelligence & information-sharing mechanisms across UK intelligence community		1,2,3	1			3-4
	Greater rights to intercept communications, especially through electronic networks		2,3	1	1	Anti-Terrorism, Crime and Security Act 2001	4-5
	FINANCE & FINANCING OF TERRORISM						
	Introduction of tough financial controls to staunch the flow of terrorist funding		2,3	All		Anti-Terrorism, Crime and Security Act 2001	4-5
	Introduction of powers for account monitoring and swift asset freezing, seizure of cash in-country, and strict reporting obligations on the financial sector including making it an offence for a bank not to report a transaction where it knows or suspects funds may be intended for terrorist purposes		2,3	All		Anti-Terrorism, Crime and Security Act 2001	4-5
	For those working in the regulated financial sector, failing to disclose where there are reasonable grounds to suspect an offence under sections 15-18 of the 2000 Act has been committed becomes an offence		2,3	All		Anti-Terrorism, Crime and Security Act 2001	4-5
	Order in Council (SI 2001 No. 3365), made under section 1 of the United Nations Act 1946 (effective 10 October 2001) empowers the Treasury to direct banks and financial institutions to freeze the accounts of individuals and entities suspected of involvement in terrorism; failure to do so is an offence.		1,2	All		As of the end of November 2001, the total amount of assets frozen in the UK stood at £77 million in 38 accounts	4-5
	Pursuant to UNSCR 1267 and 1333, accounts in the UK of those associated with the Taliban and Osama bin Laden were frozen; parallel legislation has been adopted for the Crown Dependencies and Overseas Territories		2,3	All		Prior to SI 2001 No. 3365	4-5
	Adherence to OECD Financial Action Task Force (FATF) Special 8 FATF Recommendations		1,2	All			4-5
	HEALTH, PUBLIC SAFETY and WMD						
	Measures to close the gaps in current legislation relating to chemical, nuclear and biological weapons to prevent the use, production, possession or participation in unauthorised transfers of these materials	2,4, 6	1	1		Anti-Terrorism, Crime and Security Act 2001; Chemical Weapons Act 1996	4-5
	UK's Fire Services given £53 million in new funding to give further protection to the public and emergency services in the event of a major chemical, biological or radiological attack	2,4, 6	2,3	1-5	1,2, 3	February 2002	4-5
	Biological & Chemical						
	Increased preparedness for in case of an attack utilizing biological or chemical weapons	2,4, 6	1	1-5	1		3-4
	Review of all plans for protecting the public from any possible biological or chemical attack by the Chief Medical Officer	2,4, 6	2	All	1	Anti-Terrorism, Crime and Security Act 2001	3-4

	Ensuring Doctors know how to access information from the Public Health Laboratory Service website on the signs and symptoms of anthrax	2,4, 6	2,3	All	1,2, 3	Anti-Terrorism, Crime and Security Act 2001	2-4
	Signing of an agreement with the United States on protecting citizens from bio-terrorism through the pooling of intelligence, expertise and planning	2,4, 6	1	1			5
	New safety instructions for postal workers for handling suspicious mail	2,4, 6	2,3	All	1,2, 3		2-4
	Nuclear						
	£250,000 contribution to a fund run by the International Atomic Energy Agency (IAEA), which will support activities aimed at combating nuclear terrorism	2,4, 6	1,2	1			3-5
	Introducing provisions for extending the jurisdiction for the United Kingdom Atomic Energy Authority Constabulary (UKAEAC) so that it can protect nuclear sites and nuclear material more effectively	2,4, 6	1,2	1-4	1	Anti-Terrorism, Crime and Security Act 2001	3-5
	Infrastructural/Information Assurance						
	Enhancement of existing infrastructure (including informational) security measures and agencies; integration of civil emergency planning with national infrastructure security response	All	1,2	1-2	1,2, 3	Via Civil Contingencies Secretariat (CCS) and National Infrastructure Security Co-ordination Centre (NISCC)	4-5
	Introduction of measures to enable communication service providers to retain data generated in the course of their business, namely the records of calls made and other data, not the content	All	2,3	1-2, 6	1,2, 3	Anti-Terrorism, Crime and Security Act 2001	5
FOREIGN, EUROPEAN AND INTERNATIONAL AFFAIRS							
	International co-operation to combat terrorism						
	Active participation in anti-terrorism activities of the UN, EU and other international bodies		1	1,5			5
	Full support for and implementation of UNSCR-1373 (Terrorism), UNSCR-1267 (Taliban), UNSCR-1333 (Osama bin Laden) and UNSCR-1390 (Taliban/UBL)		1	1		Externally/internationally	5
	Support for establishment of UN Counter-Terrorism Committee (CTC), currently chaired by the UK Permanent Representative to the UN Sir Jeremy Greenstock		1	1			5
	Participation in Operation Enduring Freedom		1,2	1,5			5
	Participation in UN-authorised International Security Assistance Force to promote stability in Afghanistan		1,2	1,5			5
	Adherence to OECD Financial Action Task Force (FATF) Special 8 FATF Recommendations		1	All			4-5
	Increased international assistance to states which oppose terrorist activity		1	1,5		Esp providing economic and political support to Afghanistan's neighbours to help with the burden of this conflict	3-5
	Taking immediate steps to deal with the humanitarian crisis confronting Afghanistan and to help neighbouring countries deal with the refugee problem		1,2	1,5,6			3-5
	Measures at European Union level						
	EU Action Plan against terrorism including enhanced police and judicial co-operation and strengthened air security		1	1-5			3-4
	Increased co-operation on criminal, juridical and law enforcement matters, and support for strengthening legal systems to deny terrorist sanctuary in EU		1,2	1-4			3-4
	Support for EU common list of terrorist organisations		1	1			3-4
	Creation of fast-track extradition and an EU arrest warrant		1	1-4			3-4
	Setting-up a team of EU Member States' anti-terrorist experts who can ensure timely collection and analysis of information and		1,2	1-5			3-4

	intelligence and draft threat assessments						
	Support for conclusion of the US/Europol Initial Co-operation Agreement on 6 December 2001		1	1			5
	Introducing the requirement that the potential impact on the fight against crime and terrorism is fully considered in the drafting EC legislation		1	1			4-5
	Support for strengthening of Europol		1	1-2			3-4

Belgium[83]

General overview

Background

Belgium has not been exposed to any waves of terrorist attacks for almost two decades[84]. In more recent years, the country has been subjected to acts of eco-terrorism[85], and it has also claimed some successes in dismantling a number of Kurd and Islamic terrorist groups, most visibly a Belgian branch of GIA (Armed Islamic Group)[86]. This anti-GIA effort of the late nineties played a big role in streamlining the different agencies, as by the end of June 1999, a more efficient structure was created including all relevant actors (Federal Police, State Security, AGG, general and military intelligence services, etc.).

Fig. 15 Arrest of GIA suspect in Antwerp, 7 March 1999

Belgium does not have – and will not have until the entry into force by late 2002 of the new EU framework decisions – any specific anti-terrorist legislation. Belgian legislation does not contain the concept of an 'terrorist offence', and terrorists can only be tried for the 'downstream' actual offences they commit, and not for any upstream activities. Also the security and law enforcement agencies continue to have fairly limited national instruments at their disposal to pursue alleged terrorists, although the government is trying to expand these.

Reactions to 9/11

Belgium's reaction to the events of 9/11 was affected by a number of important factors:

---

[83] In the context of this quick scan, we were unable to cover Belgium to a similar depth as the other countries that we researched. Hence, this chapter does not follow the same format as the other country chapters do.

[84] Between October 1984 and December 1985, the Marxist-Leninist 'Cellules Communistes Combattantes' (CCC – Fighting Communist Cells) perpetrated 28 bomb attacks in Belgium against NATO bases, banks and companies. The members of that organization were arrested, put on trial and convicted.

[85] Such as the Animal Liberation Front (ALF), which has claimed responsibility for a number of arson incidents in various McDonalds restaurants in Flanders.

[86] Eight members of GIA were arrested in Belgium in 1998.

- The large-scale restructuring of Belgian judicial and law enforcement structures as a result of a number of major scandals was in the process of being finalized, and had already been preceded by a large political debate on similar issues;
- Belgium happened to have the presidency of the European Union when the events started (absorbing much attention and energy from the relevant ministries)
- The apparent intention of the government not to make any decisions that would convey an impression that the country was in an emergency[87].

Possibly as a consequence of these factors, the Belgium government does not appear to have made any systematic presentation to its citizens or to the outside world about the measures it took after 9/11 in the field of counterterrorism[88].

Immediate reactions

The government ('kernkabinet') took special measures to protect Belgian air space, embassies (including NATO), the Jewish community and also the representation office of the Palestinian Authority, and international schools.

- The Belgian armed forces were put at a higher degree of readiness – from level 'Alpha' to level 'Bravo', essentially entailing increased surveillance and strengthened access control for military quarters. Four F-16 fighter-planes were also put on alert at the airbases of Florennes and Kleine-Brogel, ready to fly out within less than 15 minutes ('Quick Reaction Alert').
- Development of a European counter-terrorism action plan as president-in-office of the European Union
- Creation of a federal mixed cell for information about public order (FGCI). The FGCI was to temporarily take care of intelligence cooperation between the federal police, State Security, general intelligence service, the Antiterrorist Mixed Group ('antiterroristische gemengde groep' – AGG), the ARP and the municipal police services of the police zones involved in the events. This cell collects and analyses information pertaining to public order, including on the aspect of counter-terrorism[89].

---

[87] Very clearly in Minister Duquesne's testimony before parliament. « Qu'on ne compte pas sur moi pour utiliser des législations d'exception qui feraient croire qu'on est dans une situation d'exception.» Le ton, comme chez tous les membres du gouvernement, est à l'apaisement. La Belgique fera certes preuve de vigilance accrue sans pour autant verser dans la paranoïa. «Dans un Etat de droit, la présence de suspects sur le territoire n'est pas une raison suffisante pour prendre des mesures à caractère répressif», insiste Duquesne. On renforcera cependant l'observation et l'investigation complémentaires" « Moyens accrus contre le terrorisme ,» *La Libre Belgique*, 18/09/2001.

[88] The presentations made in the days and weeks following the attacks, for instance, were almost entirely devoted to the anti-terrorist measures the Belgian Presidency was pursuing at the EU level; with only scant attention to the strictly national measures. The (extremely sparse) website of the Federal Ministry of the Interior also has no information on these issues.

[89] The security policy after the attacks in the United States ('Het veiligheidsbeleid na de terroristische aanslagen in de Verenigde Staten van Amerika'). Report from the commission for the Interior and administrative affairs . By Willame-Boonen. Legislative document n° 2-924/1, Belgische Senaat, Zitting 2001-2002, 16 oktober 2001.

Measures undertaken within few months

- The Council of Ministers approved a special budget 7.4 mln Euro on 30 November 2001 to develop, as soon as possible, a plan to combat bio terrorism and chemical terrorism (including for the procurement of anthrax vaccines)[90].
- Threat of chemical or biological attack (hoaxes) so far is punishable by imprisonment from eight days to three months and a fine from 0.5 to 2.5 k Euro. There is a proposal to treat these threats in a similar way as threats with fissile materials, enabling imprisonment from five to ten years.

Some characteristics of the national institutional framework

There are four main agencies that are specifically engaged in counter terrorist activities:

- **The Department 'Terrorism and Sects' of the Federal Police** (second direction-general of the judicial police within the federal police), which plays a coordinating role at the federal level. It consists of three cells:
  - Cell 'Islam '(primarily engaged in the Turkish-Kurd problem);
  - Cell 'Operations', responsible for all other national and international forms of terrorism; and
  - The cell 'Sects'
- **The Mixed Antiterrorist Group** (AGG) – created in 1984 after an attack on the Brussels synagogue (1982); and beefed up in 1991 after the Gulf War. The group has some twenty staff members, and is tasked with the gathering, analysing and evaluating of the intelligence that is required for policy or legal measures. The group finds itself under the direct supervision of both the Minister of Justice and of Interior; and is independent. It is not involved in the actual investigation, but merely collects and analyses information that is then further processed by the intelligence services (both civilian and military).
- **State Security** – the law of 30 November 1998 specifies the tasks of this agency and includes an operational definition of terrorism: 'the use of violence against persons or material interests for ideological of political reasons aimed at achieving goals through terror, intimidation of threats'. The tasks of the agency include both intelligence and security. The intelligence section includes tracking espionage, interference, terrorism, extremism, proliferation, harmful sectarian organisations and organised crime.
- **The 'Terrorism and Public Order' (Terop) service of the Federal Police.** This service falls under the federal police but is a decentralized service in Brussels. It is active both in the field (tasks of the judicial police) and in the gathering of intelligence (tasks of the administrative police). The service has about forty staff, all of who also

---

http://www.senaat.be/www/webdriver?MIval=/publications/viewPub.html&COLL=S&LEG=2&NR=924&VOLGNR=1&LANG=nl.

[90] See also http://www.health.fgov.be/WHI3/krant/krantarch2001/kranttekstoct1/011012m14whi.htm.

work in the field. Its tasks are considered to require the utmost discretion and an attempt is made to avoid as much publicity as possible[91].

With respect to intelligence, the civilian intelligence services (the State Security and General Intelligence Service – 'Algemene Dienst Inlichtingen en Veiligheid', or ADIV) is responsible for the collection and analysis of terrorist information. Military intelligence services (SGR – the Intelligence Service of the Belgian MoD, made official by an organic law of 30 November 1998) can only be called upon when a certain dossier has a military aspect (e.g. the CCC attacks in the mid 80's, which included military targets). They have limited means but have a protocol agreement on exchange of information with State Security[92].

The 'Consensusnota'[93] a division of labour between different agencies, in which the 'Rijkswacht' (Federal Police) received special responsibility for counter-terrorism. Most Special Brigades of the Federal Police in large cities ('Bewakings- and Opsporingsbrigades' - BOBs) have special counter terrorist units, including the Brussels 'Cel Ter' (terrorism cell created in early 80s), some twenty staff in 1999.

Also the 'Centraal Bureau voor Opsporingen' (Central Bureau for Investigation) has a terrorism program, created in March 1997 after attacks on World Trade Centre and the Paris metro, for the coordination, support and control of counter terrorist activities within the Federal Police. It has a staff of fifteen.

There is increasing emphasis on cooperation and coordination among local and federal police forces. This has been officially announced by the Minister of Justice in the protocol agreement between state security and judicial authorities (national magistrates, instruction judges, and public prosecutors)[94].

Already prior to the events of 11 September, a number of parliamentary commissions had heightened public interest in counter-terrorism, and had led to a number of institutional changes. A Senate report in July 2001 came to the conclusion that there was too much

---

[91] Analysis of counter terrorism: legal aspects and police practices (*'Analyse van de bestrijding van het terrorisme : wettelijke aspecten en politiepraktijk')*. Report of the commsion for the interior and administrative affairs. Editor: Wille. Belgische Senaat, Zitting 2000-2001, 3 juli 2001, Legal; document n° 2-774/1.
http://www.senaat.be/www/webdriver?MIval=/publications/viewPub&BLOKNR=1&COLL=S&LEG=2&NR=774&PUID=32035&LANG=nl .

[92] Willame-Boonen Report quoted earlier.

[93] Memo of 16 april 1999: 'Omzendbrief van 16 april 1999 van het College van Procureurs-generaal bij de Hoven van Beroep betreffende de Ministeriële richtlijn van 16 maart 1999 tot regeling van de samenwerking, de coördinatie en de taakverdeling tussen de lokale politie en de federale politie inzake de opdrachten van gerechtelijke politie, door de Minister van Justitie aan de voorzitter van het College van procureurs-generaal toegezonden met het oog op de verspreiding en de inwerkingtreding op dinsdag 20 april 1999, nr. COL 6/99'.

[94] Successful cooperation ("Succesvol samenwerken")
http://www.polfed.be/old_site/rw/revue/149/149_04.htm.

overlap between these services. In response, they proposed a fundamental revision of the composition and the functioning of the 'Antiterroristische Gemengde Groep' (AGG), which had until then been tasked with synthesising the available intelligence in the fight against terrorism.

In November 2001, the Minister of the Interior Duquesne proposed to create a new 'Federal Direction for Public Security' (FDOV) – a permanent technical body charged with the collection and analysis of information about public safety, the evaluation of the danger of disturbances, and the proposal of measures or actions that would prevent or limit the consequences of such disturbances. His colleague of Justice Mr. Verwilghen appears to be opposed to such a new body, but agrees on the need for a better co-ordination of the various actors involved[95].

Conclusions

When Al-Queda struck in the USA, Belgium had the presidency of the European Union. Therefore, top representatives from Belgian government were instrumental in helping to draft the response of the Union. Also, the capacity of the Belgian government was already stretched thin because of European obligations. As a result, it was difficult for Belgium to find enough manpower to do as thorough a job on a national basis as some other countries did – or at least to inform the public about any such measures. In addition, Belgian had just seen a major restructuring of the legal institutional framework for internal security. These factors hampered Belgium's capacity to make radical changes post 9/11. Moreover, the governments' intention was to not arouse the country unnecessarily. Nevertheless, Belgium did call for extra attention to objects under threat (e.g. aviation, embassies, etc.) and in general increased intelligence, which was already focussed on heavily after recent reforms.

Belgium recognised the need to increase preparedness for biological and chemical attacks.

The relevant institutional framework was just changed prior to 9/11, decreasing the fragmentation across organisations that was noted earlier. Although additional centralisation of the responsibility and authority for counter-terrorism is under consideration, it is unlikely that this will actually take place. The Belgian Federal Police plays an important role in the fight against terrorism. This set-up naturally creates a good atmosphere for coordination. Still, the government saw reason to further improve coordination by setting up dedicated bodies with that responsibility. Belgian law does not authorize cracking down on terrorists early and vigorously. This legal situation is however expected to change soon.

---

[95] Joint meeting of the committees for the Interior and Administrative Affairs, General Affairs, Public prosecutor and Justice. ('Gemeenschappelijke vergadering van de commissies voor de Binnenlandse Zaken, de Algemene Zaken en het Openbaar Ambt en voor de Justitie van de Kamer en van de commissies voor de Binnenlandse Zaken en de Administratieve Aangelegenheden en voor de Justitie van de Senaat, dinsdag 2 oktober 2001, CRIV 50 COM 545'). http://www.lachambre.be/commissions/cri/50/3/html/ic545.htm.